THE ROMANS

in Breconshire and Radnorshire

A Field Guide

Atelier Productions

First published in 1995
by Atelier Productions
Terfyn, Glanwern, Borth, Dyfed

Reprinted 1995

ISBN 1 899793 00 3

British Library Cataloguing-in-Publication Data.
A catalogue record for this book is
available from the British Library.

Printed in Great Britain by Quacks the Booklet Printers
7, Grape Lane, York YO1 2HU   Tel. 01904 635967

CONTENTS

INTRODUCTION

The Place

That part of mid-Wales currently perceived as Breconshire and Radnorshire is criss-crossed with Roman roads connecting forts, fortlets, mansions, mines and shrines. This ghost-geography of the ancient world lies under modern roads, field-boundaries, forestry brakes, cattle yards and mountain tracks, but much of it is still visible and tangible beneath and between the hard structures of modern economies. It is there to be raised, to be visited and travelled like any other foreign geography, along its seeded roads and through its fallen gates.

The People

Few of the 'Romans' were from Rome, and the British were all Celts; the Picts had much of Scotland, the Scots were still in Ireland, and the English had not yet invented themselves. This unfamiliar ethnic arrangement was neither clear-cut at the time, nor a prime factor in the struggle between Celtic, Iron Age Britain and Imperial, classical Rome. Economics was the thing: Rome needed metals, grain and man-power. The Conquest and Occupation of Britain were both an offensive action in order to acquire these, and a defensive action to protect northern Gaul, which was already in Roman possession. These two themes, exploitative and self-protective, run through the whole four-century history of Rome in Britain, and nowhere more starkly than in Wales. Here was gold, silver, tin, lead and timber. Beef and leather, slaves, grain, hounds and gorgeous reputations were there for the taking from fractious hillsmen. But the fractious hillsmen did not give them up readily, though it is still unclear to what extent the tribes of central Wales remained mutinous through the centuries of Occupation, and how the Romans responded.

Mid-Wales was the territory of two major tribes. The Silures, a savage, dark people with curly hair and a great enthusiasm for battle, occupied the southern lands from the Bristol Channel shore northwards. The Ordovices, who held the high, mineral-rich mountains and the upper Severn valley, were so in love with bloodshed that only wholesale slaughter could be expected to curb them. The Silures were caused to accept which side their bread was buttered on, and consequently figure in Roman contexts, but the remnant of the Ordovices may have remained fractious, and proud of it, into the next era. A curious footnote to their history appears on a stone engraved around the time when Beowulf fought the Hetware. It reads: "[the stone of] Corbalengus. He lies here. An Ordovician."

ECM 126. Dated to the late 5th century, or 6th c.
Penbryn, Cardiganshire, SN 289 514.

(Letter shapes after Nash-Williams)

The Time

The Iron Age cultures of Britain were heroic, bloody, spiritual and tough. They were not composed solely of bands of grubby goatherds living in soggy mud round-houses, with a few decomposing scalps stuck on a pole over the door, any more than of Druid-haunted mystics contemplating mistletoe by moonlight. They were not united, and they were not literate, but they were in no state of decline when the Roman Conquest put an end to them.

In 55 and 54 BC Gaius Julius Caesar made his portentous but militarily unproductive assaults on the Kentish shore at Deal. During the century which followed, the upper echelons of those Iron Age societies with the closest links across the Channel developed a considerable commercial contact with Roman Gaul, and a keen appreciation of both the benefits and the hazards of becoming Roman Britain. In AD 43, after the seismic political events in Rome which established the Empire, the intellectual Claudius saw the Conquest of Britain as a way to strengthening his somewhat weedy image. The Conquest was a bloody affair, the overall outcome of which was inevitable, but the course of which was devious. The tribes responded differently to their perception of the threats and promises of Romanisation, some coming to the lure, some appreciating the hopelessness of resistance, and others holding out to the last drop of political (or arterial) blood.

One such was Caratacus, king of the British Catuvellauni, who after defeat in the east of Britain went underground and re-surfaced as resistance war-lord among the fractious hillsmen, to their and his everlasting fame. In the company of his wife, daughters and brother, this son of Cymbeline massed the Ordovices, the Silures, and all who feared Imperial 'civilisation' , on the shores of the Severn. This last, desperate battle was probably fought at, or near, Cefncarnedd (a hillfort overlooking the river at Caersws) or Dolforwyn (across it from Abermule). Here, under "a roof of locked shields", the Romans eventually dismantled his defences, slaughtered his warriors, and took his family in chains. In a final act of treachery (or realism), Caratacus himself was handed over by the queen of the Celtic Brigantes, with whom he had sought sanctuary. In chains, he was paraded through the streets of Rome like a captured king. It was then, to the Emperor Claudius, that he put the ultimate question of all unwilling colonials: "If you want to rule the world, does it follow that everyone else welcomes enslavement?" So impressed (and clever) was Claudius that the Caratacus family were accorded their freedom, and Ostorius, who had commanded the Roman army against them, a Triumph.

Despite these resonant goings-on Ostorius and his successors, Frontinus and then Agricola, were left with the continued fractiousness of the hillsmen to contain, and the mineral-rich mountains to exploit. The great roads and the grim forts are the standing monuments of that drawn-out effort which took three centuries out of Celtic history.

Key persons and dates mentioned in the text.

55 and 54 BC	**Julius Caesar's** invasions
AD 41-54	**Claudius** Emperor
43	Conquest initiated
47-52	**Ostorius** Scapula Governor of Britain
50	**Caratacus** defeated
54-68	**Nero** Emperor
61	**Boudicca** ('Boadicea')'s rebellion put down

The Flavian dynasty

69-79	**Vespasian** Emperor	
73-74, 77-78	**Frontinus** Governor of Britain	
78-84	**Agricola** Governor	*Tacitus writing history*
98-117	**Trajan** Emperor	*& Pliny writing letters*
117-138	**Hadrian** Emperor and Wall builder	

Introduction

The Antonine dynasty

138-161   **Antoninus** Pius Emperor and Wall builder

The Severan Emperors and their rivals

193-211   Septimus **Severus** (193-197 *v.* Albinus)

211-217   **Caracalla** (211-212 *v.* Geta)

260-273   The Gallic Empire

306-337   **Constantine the Great** (-323 *v.* 6 rivals)

313   Constantine directs the Empire into Christianity.

399-408   The relationship between Rome and Britain breaks up.

All dates are taken from Salway's *Roman Britain*,

Oxford History of England, Vol. 1A

This booklet is designed to be used by travellers along the known Roman roads, a section to each road. There are two main focal points - the forts at Brecon in the south and Castell Collen in the north - to and from which the roads radiate (see map). The entries are arranged as they occur along the road: thus an entry concerning a tradition of a gold coin now lost may come between a description of a major fortification and a notice of an aerial photograph which might indicate the line of a Roman road. To avoid long graphic descriptions of single fields, murky lanes and bleak expanses, all sites are pin-pointed by their National Grid Reference, and the number of the map on which they can be found. Neighbouring sites will share a map number and a route along modern roads. Old county names are given, as so many of the original reports and the National Monuments and Cadw indices refer to these, and they are no longer easy to work out on a modern map. Local government reorganisation in 1996 will reduce the south-west of Breconshire, and some of Radnorshire will be re-assigned. Alas, there is bound to be some confusion, in which the original county references can only be helpful.

Introduction

Example:

Site name	**National Grid Reference**	**OS 1:50 000 map number**	**Old county**
			(BRecon or
Alternative		(Land Ranger Series)	RAdnor etc.)

Thus:

Brecon Gaer	OS 002 297	**LR 160**	**BR**
Aberyscir			

In this guide the grid reference numbers (eastings and northings) have been separated for ease of reference.

In addition, two other number series are given for those who want to investigate further. The RIB numbers refer to the numbered entries in *The Roman Inscriptions of Britain*, vol. I, by R.G.Collingwood and R.P.Wright (Oxford, 1965). This is the definitive catalogue of inscribed stones known up to the date of publication. ECM numbers similarly refer to V.Nash-Williams' *Early Christian Monuments of Wales* (University of Wales Press, Cardiff, 1950).

*

A Roman coming into Wales during the Occupation would have to ride, or more probably march, along the great roads from fort to fort. If there was no road, he would be put to laying one; no fort, he must build one. This guide follows these Roman routes. It is divided into sections, each based on a known road and the Roman and Romano-British sites on and around it.

The road numbers used here are taken from the 1967 (revised) edition of Ivan Margary's comprehensive book, *Roman Roads in Britain*. To avoid confusion with modern road systems, Margary prefixed his numbers with RR (thus Watling Street appears as RR 6). Since then aerial photography, undaunted scholarly proddings, rescue excavation and general public enthusiasm have led to the discovery of many more ancient highways. In the National Monuments Record (NMR) of the Royal Commission on Ancient and Historical Monuments in Wales (RCAHMW), those which are certainly Roman are prefixed RRX, and those which are most probably of

Roman origin, RRN: which system has also been followed here. The NMR holds a series of key linear maps showing the known and suggested routes, and these are accessible to anyone who wishes to study the roads in detail.

This guide merely indicates where the original road can be seen or travelled in areas of public access. Anyone wishing to go further from the twentieth century can check the road on the NMR maps, and apply personally to the landowner concerned. This also applies to visiting sites where there is no public access. Many of them can be seen from the road, or after a walk along footpaths or across common land, **but many lie in working farms, and permission to see these must always be sought on an individual basis.**

A SEASONAL NOTE: Roman-tripping has two major drawbacks. In the summer the high vegetation, whether grass or bracken, makes some earthworks extremely difficult to find, though very pleasant to sit on. In the winter, when they are much easier to see (especially under a light scattering of snow or a hoar frost), they can be exceedingly chilly. A tramp along RR 62b in January will give a convincing feet-on experience of the tribulations of antiquity.

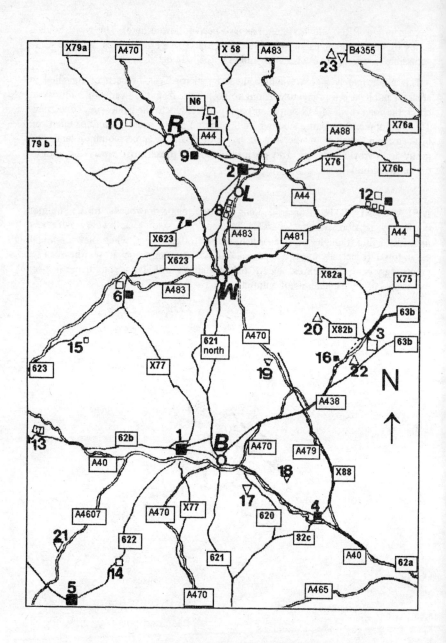

Principal Sites and Roads

KEY

■	Forts
■	Fortlets
☐	Temporary camps and other military stations
☐	Marching Camps
▽	Non-military occupation - villa, settlement etc.
△	Industrial and other sites
O	Modern towns
62b ───	Roman Road
A470 ～	Modern Road

R : Rhayader
L : Llandrindod Wells
W : Builth Wells
B : Brecon

1. Brecon Gaer
2. Castell Collen
3. Clyro
4. Pen-y-Gaer
5. Coelbren
6. Caerau
7. Penmincae
8. Llandrindod Common
9. Dolau (fort)
10. Esgairperfedd
11. Cwm-ys-y-rhiw
12. Hindwell & Walton
13. Y Pigwn
14. Ystradfellte
15. Abererbwll
16. Llowes Gaer
17. Maesderwen
18. Llan-gors
19. Llangoed
20. Painscastle
21. Ogof-yr-Esgyrn
22. Gwernyfed
23. Beguildy

Route 1 : RX 76b and RRX 75 - The Roads West from Mortimer's Cross

RR 6b & 6c, WATLING STREET west

Watling Street is perhaps the most famous of all the great Roman roads in Britain. It runs from GLEVUM (Gloucester) in the south to Carlisle and the western end of Hadrian's Wall in the north, right up the eastern border of modern Wales. Although its length is now all in England, it was from Watling Street that all Roman roads left for Wales. In the south, the RR 60a ran from the Street to ISCA (Caerleon), which was built as home base for the Second Legion Augustus (LEG II AVG), the legion responsible for the garrisons of the southern part of Wales. In the north, the Street itself passed through DEVA (Chester), base of the Twentieth Legion Valeria Victrix (LEG XX V.V.), responsible for the north. Half-way between the two legionary forts stood VIRICONIUM (Wroxeter), with its magnificent civil settlement. Today this is still a tremendous and exhilarating sight, and a salutary experience for anyone coming out of the stormy western mountains, from their punitive metal-workings and repressive forts. How much more so must it have seemed to shivering legionaries on leave from Esgairperfedd or Penmincae.

As political and military affairs fluctuated through the centuries, it was from some point on Watling Street that all troops, would-be emperors, news, supplies, and chain-gangs for the mines left or approached Wales. It has a significance for Wales which disregards all subsequent dykes and borders.

RRX 75 from Mortimer's Cross to Clyro

The road west from Mortimer's Cross divided near Shobden. The northern branch, known as RRX 76b, travelled through modern Presteigne and Bleddfa to the great fort at Castell Collen, near Llandrindod Wells in the centre of Wales. The southern branch headed down, east of Knighton, to enter modern Wales at Brilley Mountain (c.SO 267 515), on its way to Clyro.

Between these two roads, but not close to either of them, are the major installations in the Hindwell valley.

Hindwell and Walton : SO 26, SW & SE   LR 148   RA

Walton is a small hamlet and Hindwell a large farm estate just to the north of it. The large, open vale of Hindwell Brook - sunny, low-lying and east-facing - has been a harbour for herds and the men with them throughout antiquity. They left it supremely rich in hunting and occupation remains, with funerary and ritual monuments from the fifth millenium BC to the Middle Ages - especially the areas around the Summergil and Hindwell Brooks. These run into the Lugg just down-stream of Presteigne, through one of a series of valleys between the Wye and the Severn, and flow west from the Marches into the mountains of mid-Wales. Into the mountains of the Ordovices. Into this valley, in the earliest years of the Conquest, the Roman army struck.

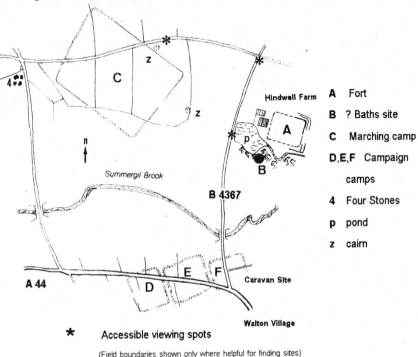

A   Fort
B   ? Baths site
C   Marching camp
D,E,F   Campaign camps
4   Four Stones
p   pond
z   cairn

*   Accessible viewing spots

(Field boundaries shown only where helpful for finding sites)

Hindwell Fort : SO 258 606   LR 148   RA

(Marked A on the sketch-map)

The muted remains of the ramparts, of which the north-east corner has the most presence, lie directly behind the buildings of Hindwell Farm, and may be seen only by personal permission from the owners.   However they can be glimpsed from the road-edge north of the farm, looking diagonally across the field from the point where the old lane makes a cross-roads with the by-road coming in from the west. An even more spectacular sight is the position of the fort's south-west corner. Here the rampart reached nearly to the edge of the huge, duck-loud pond; and although the remnant ramparts cannot be seen as such, the flat block of land where the fort stood is clear and defined beyond the water.

Unusually, more is known about the finds from Hindwell than about the fortifications. Since the fort was recognised in the late 1950s, a small section of the ditch was excavated before new farm buildings were constructed. This revealed a two-phase defence-work. The first cutting of this was V-shaped and extremely early. It seems to have been open only for a year or two, and then allowed to deteriorate before it was deliberately filled in. Some timber in the fill may hint at wooden lacing in the rampart, like that at Leintwardine, Castell Collen (q.v.) and Coelbren (q.v.).

After a short interval the invading army returned and the ditch was re-cut, deeper, wider, and to a nastier pattern. [The 'Punic' ditch worked like a ha-ha in reverse: it was impossible to climb back up the vertical outer side; those trapped in its depths came out feet first.]

Although some daub was found in the middle of the fort area, no sign of any more permanent structure could be detected in the small area available for excavation; however the presence of charcoal and iron slag in the fill of the re-cut ditch suggests that iron-working was carried on within the defences - a ballista-bolt indicates to what end. A piece of a part-silver brooch was found, and a baking oven had been built and restored just behind the rampart.

This second ditch was kept open for about a decade or so before it, too, was filled in and the ramparts levelled. Two copies of coins from the reign of Claudius, and some Samian ware dated to AD 55-70, give even the second occupation a very early date. Similarly early pottery has been found just across the modern border, in England; some turned up in the old city ditch around mediaeval Hereford and at the major military station at Leintwardine. This places the construction of the fort at Hindwell, on the threshold of Ordovician territory, at the very start of the Conquest of Wales.

The military baths (B on the sketch map) were probably situated to the south-west of the fort in the roadside field between the copse and the pond. From here, when the field was being levelled, a large number of tile, hypocaust flue and pottery sherds were collected. Debris of iron, bronze, nails, bone and ash might indicate either a baths building with its furnace, a tile kiln, or even a *mansio* like that at Brecon Gaer (q.v.), although the state of hostilities would seem to militate against the last. The finds came from one end of a large, shallow clay-lined hollow, beneath which was a deep, wide trench. The pottery represented at least twelve different vessels: some coarse everyday ware, and one Samian piece datable to the first century. A very fine piece of an amber glass jug, and bits of an amphora, certainly suggest fully developed, permanent occupation, but a test pit failed to strike any constructed building remains.

Hindwell Marching Camp : SO 250 608   LR 148   RA

(C on the sketch map)

This enormous camp, which covers forty-four acres of good farm-land in half a dozen fields, is almost entirely invisible on the ground. One entrance can be seen from the air in the centre of the eastern side. As with so many of the sites discovered from the air, the eye that knows exactly where they are is quite capable of imagining that it can detect faint colour changes on the ground. Certainly, my field-notes do say: "Very slight stains in winter crop", and include a sketch of exactly the right spot (made standing on the roof of the car in a howling wind) - but with the addendum: "Could be anything". Such is Roman-tripping.

From within the area of the camp, part of the rim of a Roman vessel was turned up by the plough in 1992.

Walton Camps : S0 251 599, 253 599, 255 599   LR 148   RA

(D, E & F on the sketch map.)

This line of three camps cannot really be seen, even from a car-roof. They lie side by side across the A44 immediately west of Walton, with the eastern-most under the caravan park. The way they are aligned, with their east and west entrances opening straight into the rampart of the next-door camp, would suggest that they cannot be contemporary; their size makes it unlikely that they are practice camps, which are usually much smaller (although very large practice works are known from the Rhine). The only finds so far published are some early coins. Perhaps they represent seasonal campaigns against the fractious hillsmen, either before or after the fort was in commission. The annual consecration of military musical instruments - trumpets, brass horns and pipes - every March suggests that this may have been the beginning of the campaigning season. Perhaps the clangour of the army drowned out the bleating of the lambs in the wild springs of the Conquest.

With the camps are three other crop-marks, all circular. The largest infringes the two westerly camps, and so cannot be contemporary. The suggestion has been made that it might be an equestrian corral or arena, and that the single circle might represent a temple - both Roman. However, the valley is rich in prehistoric monuments: the mighty Four Stones and two Bronze Age tumuli stand just beyond the outline of the marching camp. The likely interpretation of the circles is that the largest is perhaps a ditched henge, and that the other two are single and double ditched barrows.

Dolyhir Quarry (Find) : SO 2432 5799   LR 148   RA

The furthest of this group of sites, unconnected to a known road, is the spoil-heap of a quarry which produced a few Roman sherds.   Since material in a quarry-dump might come from anywhere (including the floor-boards of long-distance lorries), any further investigation would be impractical. The pottery fragments have remained in private possession.

These sites lie far to the south of RR X76, which runs past the recently 'unmasked' earthwork at Discoed, and on to Buckton and Leintwardine via Presteigne and Broad Heath in the Lugg vale. They are also very far to the north of Clyro, Clifford and RR 63b, which comes into Wales along the Wye from Kenchester, supposedly MAGNIS. Our forbears were of the opinion that it was Old Radnor, not Kenchester, which was the site of the Roman MAGNIS - Old Radnor is just down the A 44 to the west of Walton. Certainly, it would seem that an as yet unfound route must lead out of the Hindwell valley south of the River Lugg - probably to join RRX 76, which, striking off from the great street along the Marches, runs on to the Wye valley sites and into the dark heart of Silurian country.

Beyond the tumulus at SO 247 500, RRX 75 is met by the track from Little Mountain, and by another road, RR 82a, which has swung in a north-hand bow from Builth Wells, where RR 621 (north) crosses the Wye half-way between the great forts of Brecon Gaer and Castell Collen - a geographically credible link, although there is no proof on the ground for the road itself. It is only fair to say that this area is not the best for Roman-tripping: the sites are of dubious Roman pedigree, and the roads are somewhat hypothetical.

Little Mountain : SO 216 496   LR 148   RA

(Also known as **The Gaer, Newchurch**)

This is labelled 'Lost' in several indices which we have seen (though presumably not because it refers to half an acre of land at nearly 1,200 feet above sea level on a bare, severely grazed hill-top). There are paths which surround the hill, but none goes directly to the site. The gentlest approach is by the marked bridle-way from Dolbedwyn Farm, on the south-west side of the hill. Permission to go off the path, and through the fields, must be asked from the farmhouse.

The site itself consists merely of two banks with a ditch between them. There is one entrance only, on the north-east side. Most authorities take the enclosure to have been post-Roman, perhaps a stock-corral; however it has typically Roman rounded corners, and some archaeologists have seen a possible *clavicula* in the bumps around the causewayed entrance. One suggestion is that if it was a Roman structure it may have been a signal post (like Gibbet Hill, Montgomeryshire), from which smoke and bonfire signals were relayed between forts set lower down in the river-valleys.

There is a possible Roman road, walkable now as a footpath, running east from the earthwork. Taken as part of RRX 75, it continues east along Red Lane before dropping south to the RR 63b at Rhydspence. Another possible branch-line of RRX 75 goes south from Little Mountain as a footpath through Crowther's Pool and Lwyngwylyn, a short length of a modern by-road, and another path down behind Court Evan Gwynne. Whilst this might suggest that Y Gaer was served by a Roman transport system, it need mean no more than that later stockmen found the old roads useful for driving cattle along... if, indeed, the roads were there in the first place.

Class Llanshiver Hill : SO 2040 4750   LR 148   RA

The older workings in these ancient lead-mines are generally attributed to Roman activity, but the dating of mine-workings is fraught with problems, and perhaps a question mark should be held in the mind, if not in the imagination. Since the Romans did extract a great deal of metal from the Welsh mountains - indeed, came specifically to get it - such workings as *may* well be Roman are often taken *as* Roman unless proved otherwise. Since proving them not to be Roman can be as tricky as proving that they are (mining, of its very nature, being a process which removes rather than preserves), the learned journals become almost combustible when the subject is brought out for an airing.

There is an earthwork beside the old mines which is quite visible, even from the minor roads circling the hill. It is difficult to reach, as the footpaths marked on the map are discouragingly unmarked on the ground. It is set in a little hollow at a spring-head, has a single, simple entrance and, in places, two ditches. It is often labelled 'Roman', but is not the best place to go to for authenticity.

From the B 4594, which curves round the west side of the hill, there is a provocative view across the wet valley of Rhos Goch to Class Llanshiver. Boggy underfoot, blind, ideal for ambush and terrorist attack, this is exactly the sort of terrain which the Roman roads rode high to avoid. In his histories of the Conquest, written around the turn of the second century, Tacitus remarks on the bogs and mires out of which the British struck, and the guerilla tactics which wrought such frequent havoc. Later, under the Occupation, the grain tax levied on the local population to feed the army and the civil administration, and the efficient agricultural methods employed by the Romans, combined to bring heavier soils into cultivation; and some of this wildwood vanished under the Roman axe. Nonetheless, many of the remote cwms and marshy river-valleys of the hinterland must have been left much as Rhos Goch is today: a guerilla's haven.

RRX 75 joins up with RR 63b for the last couple of miles to the (absolutely real) campaign fort at Clyro.

Route 2 : RR 63b - The Road to Brecon Gaer from MAGNIS (Kenchester)

This is a well recognised military road which strikes off from Watling Street at MAGNIS, just west of Hereford. It takes what is now a modern side-road, and can be travelled again on a stretch of the A 438 from Byford Common to near Willersley. The full length of the road is not proven but seems to have followed the route of the modern road to near Hay Bridge.

Joined by RRXs 75 and 82a near Court Evan Gwynne, RR 63b crossed the Wye at an unknown spot near Hay Bridge, and so to Clyro. None of this is visible, and (inevitably) alternative lines are suggested for both RRs 63b and X75, with variant junction points.

Clifford : SO 245·458   LR 148   Herefordshire

In AD 52, after Caratacus' defeat and removal to Rome, a legionary force suffered a considerable loss somewhere near Clifford or Clyro. The legion concerned was probably the Twentieth (LEG XX V.V.), one of the four core legions involved in the Conquest of Britain. [It was probably after their part in the Roman revenge on Boudicca (Boadicea) that they were granted the honour 'Victrix'.] It is possible that part of the legion was engaged in constructing the first military station at either Clifford or Clyro when it was cut off. The commander, with no less than eight centurions and "the pick of the men", fell in the ambush. The perpetrators were probably a combination of the fearsome and resilient Ordovices, and the more recalcitrant part of the Silures. Shortly after these humiliating reverses a Roman foraging party was chased from the field, and a cavalry rescue-squad put to flight. This continued resistance shocked Rome, and Ostorius, the commander who had defeated Caratacus, brought in the legionaries in strength.

The Silures were immediately threatened with transplantation or extermination by Ostorius, who was the governor of the Province of Britain at the time. Such vengeance was recognised Roman practice, not a knee-jerk reaction. The Silures retaliated by capturing two cohorts of auxiliaries. These prisoners they then 'distributed' amongst their neighbours as a live advertisement of what could be gained by joining the fray.

Ostorius collapsed with nervous exhaustion and died; the Silures took on a whole legion (the Twentieth again?) and routed them. From Rome, the Emperor Claudius despatched one governor who attempted some punitive forays before he, too, suddenly died and was hastily replaced by Didius Gallus, flushed with success in the Crimea. He found the Silures on the rampage "among the woods and bogs", but managed to curb them. Unfortunately Tacitus, who described these lively events, did not like Didius, so the elderly general's methods are unrecorded. It may be that Didius' long years of experience amongst enraged natives proved more effective than Ostorius' vengeful sword.

Clyro Camp : SO 2290 4340   LR 148   RA

Today this enormous campaign camp is blanketed by grass, and shows up among the fields as a series of heavy banks and a rolling hollow which was once the ditch. These muted remains, including one of the typically rounded Roman corners, can be seen on the left (west) bank of the river from the Hay Bridge end of the Wye Valley Footpath. There is also a good long-distance view from the B-road to Clifford, just south of the Children's Bookshop. The camp spreads through several of the fields belonging to Boatside Farm, which stands in its southern corner, and inquiries about visiting the banks must be made at the farm.

Built in the 50s and 60s, Clyro camp covers about 26 acres, and seems to have been in use only during the Conquest. Unlike many stations founded in these hectic early years, it was never replaced by a permanent, stone-built fort. The ramparts surround an area large enough to protect a full half-legion (about 2,500 regular infantry), which would amount to an eighth of the entire legionary force in Britain at the time. This would have meant a very costly reduction in the strength of any one legion, wherever it was based, in a period of considerable uncertainty. Given this, and the degree of guerilla-style resistance which the native Celts offered, it is considered more likely that Clyro was used as a base for a number of different auxiliary units, including cavalry. Excavations in 1964 showed that the defence-works were altered and re-designed, adjusting to changing troop-requirements as the progress of the Conquest fluctuated. The same 4 m. wide ditch, in places

Sextus Valerius Genialis was buried near Cirencester after twenty years' service in the Thracian cavalry, which saw action in Wales in the early years of the Occupation. The tombstone, now in Corinium Museum, Cirencester, is thought to date from the late first or early second century.

cut right into the underlying rock, served as an outer defence to two successive turf ramparts. The earliest of these was revetted on both sides with heavy timbers, but when it was rebuilt the bank was two metres wider, without any facing. Inside, the cooking ovens and part of a metalled road were found, but no permanent structures. All the finds were of Conquest date, including some Samian ware and an early wine-flagon.

It must have been an awe-inspiring sight, this alien army encamped in over three hundred identical leather tents meticulously disposed behind a massive precision-built earthwork. Today the site emanates a dulled deliberation as if, in its placid, pastoral contours, it still holds the shadows of the horse lines and the stone streets, the echoes of armourers, buglers, smiths and high-ranking officers dining among their wine flagons and Samian bowls beneath the guard patrolling high on the rampart walkways.

It would be forgivable if, in the dark nights of the Conquest, a passing Ordovician bard doubted the precise meaning of *PAX ROMANA*.

Clyro ?camp : SO 225 430   LR 148   RA

Aerial photographs show two ridges joined by a rounded corner on the same hill as Clyro camp. It is thought that this is a marching camp, possibly in emergency use before, or while, the large campaign camp was built. At a stretch of the imagination, it might very well be the site of the fateful ambush. It is not visible from the Wye Valley Footpath.

The area around Clyro and Hay-on-Wye presents difficulties of space and time. The camp at Clyro was occupied only during the Conquest, and was closed down early on, but the later sites in the area must have been connected to maintained roads. RRXs 75, from Mortimer's Cross, 82a to Builth Wells and 82b to Painscastle may be connected with later sites, but they appear to converge at Clyro, where there is at present no evidence of a contemporary cross-roads fort or fortlet to serve them.

RRX 82b : Clyro to Painscastle

This is an ancient route which may well have Roman origins. It ran north-west from the area of Clyro camp to the known site at Painscastle. It is not visible anywhere along its length, but its line is represented by side-roads and footpaths from Lloyney (c.SO 200 446) to half a mile short of Painscastle - c.SO 177 460 - where it joins the modern by-road at the approach to the village.

Painscastle : SO 166 462   LR 148   RA

At the north-west corner of the castle taken by Walter Scott as the *Garde Doloureuse* of mediaeval Arthuriana, some nineteenth century workmen dug into a tessellated floor. Once its delicate beauty was revealed, it was perceived to be a 'fairy pavement', and hurriedly re-interred lest its exposure cause dispute between the Worlds. Since the site was once known as 'Caer', and stands at a cross-roads, the Roman genesis of Painscastle was immediately appreciated by more secular minds. An ambiguous site, it has been variously interpreted as a villa, a Romano-British dwelling of high status, and a shrine.

One of the noticeable things about Roman 'Wales' is the lack of evidence for the rural shrines which played a significant part in the socio-religious activities of the Mediterranean Empire. This may reflect a sense of insecurity felt by the Romans, who had strong ideas about exposing the sacred to damage or desecration - a view obviously shared by some in the last century. The relationship between a Roman and both the spirits of place (*genii loci*), and of his own ancestral dead, was constant and strong.

Painscastle is perched aloft on a bluff overlooking a stream with rolling pasture-land behind. It is at least possible that some healing (or at least participating) spirit may have been located here: one perhaps originally deferred to by native Celts, whose divinities had long been associated with springs and rivers.

A considerable degree of Romanisation must have been achieved by the time tessellated flooring was in the sample-book for west of Watling Street. Its existence here, among the lumpy hills behind the Usk, argues a site of some standing, whether secular or sacred.

RR 63b is usually thought to have crossed the Wye near the present Hay Bridge. William Camden, a restless Elizabethan antiquary, recorded in 1586 that he had been told of coins being found in the town. Camden amassed a wealth of material for his Choreographic Descriptions of the Flourishing Kingdoms..., which archaeologists regularly mine in their research into the histories of sites.

The road went on south-west to Bronllys along the line of the A 438 to Brecon. There is no visible evidence of its Roman origins, and some authorities favour a route down the left (west) bank of the Wye, which is here turned northwards in a great loop. There are as many sites on the left bank as there are on the right. They are here divided into two groups.

LEFT BANK
Llowes Castle Tump : S0 1909 4069   LR 161   RA

This squarish earthwork, which may be Roman, is set right down on the Usk flood plain, where a *motte* is marked on the map. The site is definitely not on view, but its position, among a clump of trees at the end of a private lane, can be appreciated from the road. Further up-stream, where RR 623 crosses the Wye, the fort at Penmincae (q.v.) is set similarly close to the river.

Llowes Gaer : SO 1742 4178   LR 161   RA

This is a rectangle of cropmarks and almost imperceptible ridges in the fields adjacent to Gaer farm. They can sometimes just be picked out from a short distance below the farm, when the grass is scant and the sun low. The farm is reputed to have been built on a "defensive site of considerable magnitude", for which there is little published and no archaeological evidence, although the name 'Gaer' is suggestive. It is now guarded by extremely vigilant dogs.

Dderw Mound (find) : SO 1386 3748   LR 161   BR

On the excavation of a 'tump' here in 1978, a single, battered Roman sherd was said to have been recovered from the old ground surface. The Romans liked tumuli; they poked around in many of them, and frequently seem to have dropped their money. It was customary, in their own funerary rites, to deposit grave-goods with their dead; perhaps they left coins, or other symbolic offerings in prehistoric barrows out of superstition rather than untidiness.

Llangoed (?record) : SO 113 394   LR 161   BR

It is possible that there may have been a Roman estate centred at Upper Llangoed, overlooking the Wye valley, and some distance from the RR 63b. Experts working on the very earliest pre-Norman land charters have found evidence of groupings of large areas of farmland passed on through sale, gift and inheritance at dates not far removed from immediately post-Roman times. These lands appear to have been established as units, or parts of a unit, before the charters record their transmission. The historians have suggested that such large agricultural 'blocks', already established by this time, may derive from the previous existence of a Roman estate.

A wealthy Roman might have large villa-farms in several different parts of the Empire; there were Imperial estates; outside the larger forts were the military *prata*, defined tracts of pasture for the army's stock; retiring soldiers and administrators might receive grants of farmland as marks of favour or reward. Any of these types of tenure could form the basis of just the sort of agricultural 'unit' with which the early charters are concerned.

Such establishments could only come into being in a period when there was a sufficiently stable labour force to work them, and a socio-political context in which they were appropriate - perhaps the late third century, when the Empire had more trouble with the Germans on the continent than with the insular Celts. Once established, however, each integral tenancy could well be expected to remain intact for many generations.

Pen yr Wrlodd : SO 2248 3986   LR 161   BR

Early in this century, during the examination of a cairn (probably a neolithic long-barrow), some outside treasure-hunters turned up a considerable number of blue beads, which may be Roman, and a coin of Crispus, one of the many claimants to the imperial title early in the reign of Constantine the Great in the fourth century. Their relationship to the barrow is, understandably, unknown. "Unfortunately," an early commentator says frigidly, "the excavation was not carried out with much regard for method." In fact, the most interesting finds were made in the spoil-heaps. [Note: This is not the long barrow impeccably excavated in 1972 at SO 151.316.]

RIGHT BANK

If the Roman road travelled down the right bank of the Wye, from Hay due south, it would have passed very close to a different group of sites.

Coed y Polyn : SO 179 385   LR 161   BR

In the first years of the seventeenth century Edward Lhuyd, a migratory historian, set himself a parish-based questionnaire which he travelled around finding answers for. These Accounts of the Parishes were published in modern format as *Parochialia*. It was Lhuyd's ambition to write an entire *Archaeologia Britannia*. This was not to be, however his 'Parishes' can be enjoyed in *Archaeologia Cambrensis, 1909-11*, and contain many glittering lures for the modern antiquarian. One such is a record of (Roman) tiles being found at Coed y Polyn, suggesting a civil settlement. Alas, nothing has ever turned up since.

Gwernyfed Bloomeries : SO 1711 3724   LR 161   BR

In 1951 archaeologists were called in when Roman material was found in the holes being dug for new goal-posts in the school playing fields.

Excavation revealed an iron-working site in the field south of Felindre Brook, behind the recently-built housing estate. An iron chisel and iron fragments amidst a litter of slag, lead and charcoal were recovered from among and around the remains of four Roman furnaces. Beyond the existence of bloomeries and forge, it is not known what sort of site this was: whether it was purely industrial, or associated with a military installation. A datable sherd of Samian ware and an amphora show that it was operational in the late first century, during the early years of the Occupation.

Route 2

There is a 'Settlement' marked on the map just above, and north of, the bloomeries. This is a Celtic hillfort defended by multiple ditches in a manner typical of the end of the Iron Age (which the Conquest brought about). Excavations here in 1958 uncovered several unusual and vivid details. These included a peculiarly narrow entrance, heavily worn by excessive use, and the intriguing likelihood of a drawbridge over a defensive ditch which ran right across the gateway. This ditch had been cleaned out and recut very shortly before it was deliberately filled with material from the facing of the rampart. In the top of this debris was a pottery sherd of the same date as those in the bloomeries below. The implication is that Celtic fighting-men raiding out of the hillfort were overwhelmed by the Imperial army, and their stronghold razed.

Down below, the victors set up their iron-workings by the stream, and forged their javelin heads and arrow heads, horse-shoes and nails in readiness for the next assault. This is one of the very rare instances where activities on a given Roman site can be demonstrably related to events in a specific neighbouring Celtic fortress.

At Bronllys **RRX 89** *struck off north-west behind Llyswen for Builth Wells, but the trail goes cold in the uplands above Argoed (c. SO 091 452), and it has not been verified anywhere along its line. At Bronllys itself, the existence of an oddly rectangular bailey has led to the suspicion that Roman and Norman invaders may have found tactical advantages on the same spot. So far there is no proof for this as a Roman site, but some archaeologists feel strongly that the army should have had a fortlet here...*

Pontithel (find):   c. SO 164 366   LR 161   BR

A coin was found here in 1961, dating from the reign of Antoninus Pius - he who took so many of the troops up to Scotland in the mid second century, to build the frontier Wall north of Hadrian's.

Ty Du (find) : SO 18 34   LR 161   BR

A cairn was examined. A hoard of Roman coins was found. Time passed, and the two events became linked. The hoard resembles a later collection rather than the life savings of a nervous Roman - but upon what occasion it might have been thrust into a Bronze Age tumulus is a mystery. The metal of coinage which was not legal tender was used in later periods for its value either as bullion or for melting down and re-working.

From Bronllys, RR 63b continues south, more or less along the route of the modern A 470 to Felinfach, along a by-road to Llandew and so into Brecon east of the Cathedral. Here it joined the RR 62a for the last three miles west to the great auxiliary fort at Brecon Gaer (q.v.)

Route 3 : RR 62a - The Road up to Brecon Gaer from ISCA (Caerleon).

This is the direct road from the legionary base at ISCA to Brecon Gaer. Before Frontinus instigated the fort at BANNIUM (Abergavenny) for LEG II AVG, there had been a winter base at BURRIUM (now Usk). The Twentieth Legion Valeria, who were probably awarded the 'honour' of being known as Victrix after their part in crushing the Celtic queen Boudicca's blazing revolt, were stationed at BURRIUM at the time of the initial clashes of the Conquest. However the site was ill-chosen, and after a series of inundations the dynamic Frontinus brought LEG II AVG to the haughty bluff selected by the Normans a thousand years later for Abergavenny castle. LEG XX V.V. moved north and west with Agricola, and were finally based at DEVA (Chester).

RR 62a ran through the old station at Usk to Abergavenny, and from there up the Usk valley, along much of the line of the modern A 40, to Brecon. Having the significance of an arterial highway, it must always have been well maintained. Major road-works are known to have taken place in the reigns of Constantius Chlorus (AD 305-6) or Constantine II (337-40).

BANNIUM :   SO 30 14   LR 161   Monmouthshire

Abergavenny Castle Museum

Although it is just outside Breconshire, the castle museum has an excellent Roman exhibition with a wide range of military, domestic, luxury and coin finds from *BANNIUM* and its recently explored *vicus*. Like all military sites in Breconshire, *BANNIUM* was garrisoned by *LEG II AVG*, or units under their command. The coins and querns, glass flasks and wine flagons, cooking pots and oil-lamps in the cases here were the possessions of the same men who marched across the bleak heights above Ystradfellte, and looked out into the dangerous night from the towers of Castell Collen.

Such was the efficiency of trade and transport within the Empire that many of the

---

Route 3

pieces here will have belonged to people moving between any of the military and civilian settlements from Anglesey to Alexandria. Military stations and civilian estates in the backlands of Wales were occupied and supplied by men and goods from all over the geographic enormity of the Empire. The detailed accounts of the places of manufacture of many of the fascinating pieces in the museum emphasise the cohesion of 'Romanity'.

Garn Goch (find) : SO 2123 1771   LR 161   BR

The road runs up the left (north) bank of the river. On the opposite side, at Llangattock, six coins from the reign of Constantine I (AD 306-37) were recorded in the mid-nineteenth century. The coins are said to have been "washed out of a Bronze Age cairn". Granted that there may never have been much opportunity for frivolous spending north of Severnside, there does seem to have been an inordinate amount of 'depositing' in the queasy years of the early fourth century. The mound was given barrow-status when bones were revealed to the startled labourers of the Duke of Beaufort, who were clearing what had been taken to be an untidy heap of stones in his Grace's demesne. It is not clear, in the mid-nineteenth century account, whether the monument was the chamber of a long barrow or the cist of a cairn.

Ty Llys, Tretower : SO 1859 2128   LR 16   BR

RIB 401

There is a Roman inscription on a stone built into the garden wall of this house in the village, which is on the line of RR 62a. This 'Building Stone' is about three foot from the ground near the corner where the house meets the west boundary wall, on

(Letter shapes after Nash-Williams)

the left, looking from the road. It cannot be seen without asking the occupier for permission to come into the garden. Even when pointed out, it is not exactly flagrant. It reads: "c Peregrini fec(it)" (The Century of Peregrinus built this). The back-to-front C indicates a Century, as opposed to a personal name. The stone, thought to have originated in Pen-y-Gaer fort, was once built into the orchard wall of Tretower castle before it was re-used at Ty Llys. It refers to a length of wall (Pen-y-gaer rampart?) constructed by the unit of which Peregrinus had command. The century took its name from units of ten tents under a commander, the centurion. The tents actually served eight men, not ten, so a full century was eighty infantry, not a hundred. The building of set stretches of fort defences by each century or platoon was established practice, and accounts for the speed and standardisation of rampart construction. Here is recorded the name of one actual man, serving as a centurion, during the consolidation of the Occupation. Peregrinus really was here.

Tretower House, Tretower : SO 184 216   LR 161   BR

RIB 402

[See photograph on page 40.]

Another inscription, recording the labours of the century of Valens, is rather bizarrely built into the north gate-pier of the entrance drive. Unfortunately it is on the inside, facing the garden; and worse, it is upside down. However it is refreshingly clear and easy to read, about four feet above the ground. For anyone who has visual problems, this stone is clearly cut and very good to feel: "**C Valentis**" - The century of Valens (built this).

This, too, is likely to have come from Pen-y-Gaer.

From the end of the village street here, just beside the castle, a footpath follows RR 62a part of the way towards Pen-y-Gaer fort, less than a mile to the north west.

Pen-y-Gaer Fort : SO 169 219   LR 161   BR

Also known as **Cwmdu**

This is a grim little fort now gripping two farm-houses within its formidable stone ramparts. These are startlingly visible, even from the little by-road which runs through them, probably on the old Roman north-south gate line. Half the size of Brecon Gaer or Abergavenny, it seems likely that Pen-y-Gaer was designed for five hundred infantry in the time of Frontinus' reduction of the Silures, about AD 75. It is curiously sited, backed up against a steep hill, but it does sit up on the crest of a rise, well up above the stream. The river course runs, even now, through a tangle of willows and hazel; marshy and dark, this must be very like all the little cwms and hidden clefts which gave shelter to the beleaguered Silures. When Frontinus came, such tanglewood would be instantly cleared, and the great roads laid through wasted, open tracts with no cover for ambush parties. RR 62a crosses RRXs 88 and 82c at Pen-y-Gaer; the devastation must have seemed enormous.

A part of the defences was excavated in 1968, when a small trench and cutting were opened just to the east of the modern road where it crosses the north side of

---

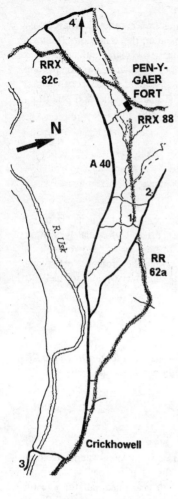

RRX 82c

PEN-Y-GAER FORT

N

RRX 88

A 40

R. Usk

RR 62a

Crickhowell

1. RIB 401   3. Garn Goch
2. RIB 402   4. Bwlch

the fort. [The likely-looking lane straight up the hill behind the fort is not a candidate for Roman status: the gradient is too steep for the transport.] The trenches revealed an early turf and timber rampart, probably part of Frontinus' conquest strategy. New forts were inspected by very senior officers, and it is quite likely that the energetic governor came here himself. A coin of the lubricious Nero, whose astonishing profile can be studied in Abergavenny Museum, turned up in the top-soil. About ten years old when it was lost, it must at some time have been dragged up from the Roman levels by a plough, rabbit or tree-root. However Gaulish Samian ware, some rather more mundane cooking pots and part of a *mortarium* were securely buried in the fort remains. The *mortarium* is made of a lovely cream-coloured ware which is thought to have come from the official army kilns in Kent. It is very smooth to touch, and while Samian ware feels like silk to the fingers, these pale *mortaria* are like well-ironed linen. The earliest levels at *ISCA, LEG II AVG*'s permanent base, have produced similar bowls.

The turf and timber station was replaced with a stone wall. This was subsequently demolished, and the material was used to construct a berm between a new, steeply-cut ditch and a yet higher wall. It was probably stretches of this that were built by the centuries of *LEG II AVG* under Valens and Peregrinus. There was insufficient evidence to give firm dates for the closure of the fort, which may have been the result of Hadrian's taking the troops up north to build the great frontier Wall which bears his name. For whatever reason, Pen-y-Gaer was closed down by AD 140. Curiously, a second Building Stone (RIB 1347) has survived at Benwell (Northumberland), where a stretch of the Wall is thought to have been built by the detachment of *LEG II AVG* brought up for the purpose. Here, too, a century of Peregrinus laboured among the stones: most likely the same men with the same tools. In such nice little quirks of archaeology do real ghosts tell tales.

The exceptional fertility of the little valley probably accounts for the presence of the two farms, and the consequent smothering of the inside of the fort. However aerial photographs have revealed a small, squarish building, suggestive of the *Principia*, under the farm buildings, and traces of what may have been barracks and granary also show up in the northern part of the fort. It has been suggested that a suspicious quarried area behind Maes Llechau, by the stream, would be a likely site for the baths, and old reports of human bones in a curious structure hint that some sort of ossuary may have existed outside the eastern defences. Pottery and pieces of dressed 'Bath' stone found in the last century hint at a settlement out along the *BANNIUM* road.

At the beginning of the nineteenth century Richard Colt-Hoare, who edited a translation of Giraldus Cambrensis on his way to becoming Founding Father of modern archaeology, reported a macabre little tale. The farmer at Pen-y-Gaer was turning up a quantity of fine glazed pottery in one of his fields. Roman burial rite in the first and early second centuries was usually cremation, and it was mandatory to locate cemeteries outside each town or fort. It is likely that the pots were in fact cremation urns from the burial ground north of the fort. These the impoverished peasantry of Colt-Hoare's day beseeched the farmer to give them - for keeping their milk in. One wonders whether the tradition of leaving out milk in earthenware pots to avert ill-luck may have anything to do with a connection between such pots and the bits of human bone which they originally contained.

Bwlch (find) : SO 1483 2208   LR 161   BR

A British copy of a coin of Claudius turned up here in 1980. Copies were not necessarily forgeries: they were often struck when there was insufficient coinage available to pay the troops. The army was prone to voting in a more generous emperor when the present incumbent failed to pay up.

At c.SO 076 274, RR 62a meets with the RR 620, which has come northwards up the east flank of Llanfigan from more or less the crossing between the two reservoirs of Pentwyn and Pontsticill. Here it joined RR 621 coming from Pen-y-Darren. It is not visible, but minor roads and tracks follow much of its theoretical line.

Millbrook Milestone : [SO 087 272] LR 160   BR

RIB 2258 & 2259   Now in Brecon Museum

The two-sided inscribed stone block was noticed set as a step into the granary of the farm. Broken in modern times, it had already been reduced and bevelled in the period between the two episodes of carving. The first side reads **IMP C/FL VAL C/ONSTA/NTIUS** (to the Emperor Caesar, Flavius Valerius Constantius). Father of Constantine the Great, Constantine I ('Chlorus') ruled from AD 293-306. He was in Britain twice, and was responsible for much reorganisation and possibly a great deal of magnificent building dated to his and/or his son's reign. The second time, he conducted a penetrative campaign against the Picts of furthest Scotland. How far he got is unclear, but he returned to York in some degree of victory and died there, leaving his son to be proclaimed Emperor in York in 306. It took Constantine many years, many pretenders and more than one God to emerge as Constantine the Great, first Christian Emperor of the Roman world.

The later inscription (RIB 2259), on the reduced side of the stone, is dedicated to Constantine the Great's second son, Constantine II, and is an inelegant piece of work.

At the north end of RR 620 at Llanfrynach, just south of its junction with RR 62a, is the only archaeological site in the area that is taken to be part of a villa.

Maesderwen Baths SO 069 258 LR 160 BR

Also known as **Llanfrynach Villa**

There is nothing to see today but a dreamy field by a small stream, some ancient trees shading fat, summer horses, and a small, elegant house looking out across ageing steeple-chase fences set in the neat cut-and-laid hedges of the Usk valley. It says much for the *genius loci* that Maesderwen is still hauntingly placid, still profoundly 'landed': to be entitled, perhaps, *'Nostalgia*, by Lionel Edwards'.

This is the site of the only likely Roman villa in the area. Only a fraction of it has ever been seen. The baths suite of what would have been a large and possibly very beautiful residence was discovered when, in 1783, the removal of a large ash tree revealed mosaic-floored rooms beneath its roots. In 1950 a modern account of the eighteenth century records was published with a plan based on the original drawings.

The datable coins (including one of Constantine I and another as late as the AD 370s) retrieved from under the tree roots suggest that the villa may have been founded in the 260s and 70s, the reigns of the 'Gallic' Emperors, when Britain was part of a deviant 'Roman Empire' which emerged in the north-west after a period of military and political horrors on the continent. The seat of this short-lived micro-empire was in Gaul, and Britain was both close and precious. The pandemonium to east and south did not affect Britain physically, but its effects were portentous. At one point the Alamanni of Germany surged as far south as Milan before they could be halted. This caused a justifiable attack of nerves in Gaul, which was itself attacked in 276 and recovered in a very shaky condition. A new and vigorous central government put a (possibly bloody) end to the Gallic Empire, and the subsequent decades were remarkable all over England for the building and beautifying of villas. The suggestion is that Gaulish landowners moved in person into Britain, either as new purchasers or because they already had land here. It looks as if Maesderwen villa may have come into being as part of this movement of persons, wealth and expensive ideas about interior decoration.

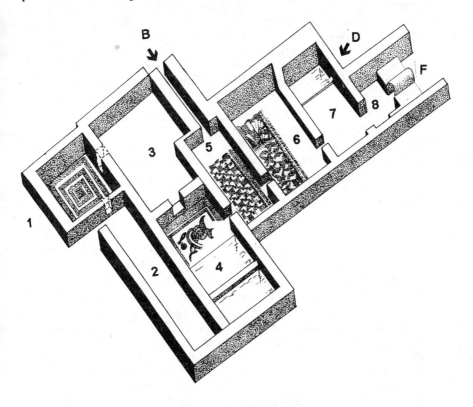

**Impression of Maesderwen baths, based on Charles Hay's plan, 1785
(republished by Nash-Williams in 1950).**

1.	Ante-chamber	5.	Warm Room	B	Booster Furnace?
2.	Passage	6.	Hot Room	D	Drain
3.	Undressing Room	7.	Hot Bath/Sweat Room	F	Furnace (+ stoking-
4.	Cold Bath	8.	Heating Room		pit and fire-hole)

Hypocaust under Sweat, Hot and Warm Rooms. Function of rooms attributed as in Nash-Williams. Entrances from the ante-chamber are guess-work by the present author, as none were shown on the eighteenth-century plan.

Roman drains, baths, hypocausts and lavatories are assumed to exercise a powerful attraction for Roman-trippers. This expectation dates, perhaps, from those hygienically-challenged and inadequately-heated Victorian days when Agricola the Genocide was taken as a model colonial governor, and is fortified in our lifetime by images of all those pink, naked Romans lolling about amongst the precise engineering. The astonishing thing about Maesderwen, however, is less the stacks of flue-tiles under the floor than the mosaics laid upon them. Distinct 'schools' of mosaicists have been distinguished in Britain. The Corinian (Cirencester) workshop, thought to have originated before the end of the third century, was the finest in the west of Britain, and is believed to have been responsible for the work at Llanfrynach.

The eighteenth-century drawing of the mosaic floors under the Maesderwen ash-tree is not very clear. It has been suggested that the draughtsman did not fully understand his subject - he certainly did not represent any inequality of preservation in the thousands of little square pieces in the mosaics, with the result that what must have been distortions and (possibly) repairs appear as variations integral to the designs. There are inconsistencies, too, in the architecture: the west doors leading out of the Cold Room and Hot Room line up exactly, whereas the door between them, linking Warm Room to Hot Room, is off-set; the north walls of the vestibule and of the first (undressing) room are very slightly stepped, and the doors between these rooms and the passage-way are not integral - the wall-base carries on without a break, as if the doors were inserted into existing walls.

Whether these oddities are attributable to Roman alterations or to eighteenth-century excavation practices is not clear, but what does emerge is the irregularity of the geometric mosaics. It looks very much as if the baths were altered, and two of the four mosaics cut off in mid-pattern as a result. Moreover, despite the fact that it is complete, the design laid in the Hot Room covers only half the floor-area, but would fit nicely into the Warm Room on its left. Here the design is incomplete - a self-repeating series of white Ls on a blue ground reminiscent of the Corinian blue and white geometric floor at Chedworth. If the Maesderwen floor had carried on, would it have lain, one has to wonder, neatly in the total area of the Hot Room? And if so, have we here an act of classical vandalism, or the efforts of imitators of the Corinian school, getting their mosaics in a tangle? No such transposition, however, can account for the slicing of the 'Dolphin' mosaic in the Cold Room. Here it seems that a second cold bath was dug into a previously laid floor, though for what reason is unimaginable, since the eighteenth century account represents both cold baths without distinction. There may have been a time-lapse between the two which was not obvious to the Georgian antiquarian, but which might explain some of these discrepancies.

It has to be said that the patterns themselves are not amongst Britain's finest. As they were recorded at the time of discovery, only the small square geometric design in the vestibule appears to be totally successful, and it does look rather as if that room was a later addition - perhaps the floor was laid by a more experienced hand. The (halved) 'Dolphin' design in the Cold Room is somewhat bitty - a fish with *rigor mortis* (an appropriate bathroom motif or a Christian symbol?), and a sand-worm's upcast (a shell?) fail to integrate convincingly with the nether-end of what may be two intertwined sea-snakes. Depending on the accuracy of the

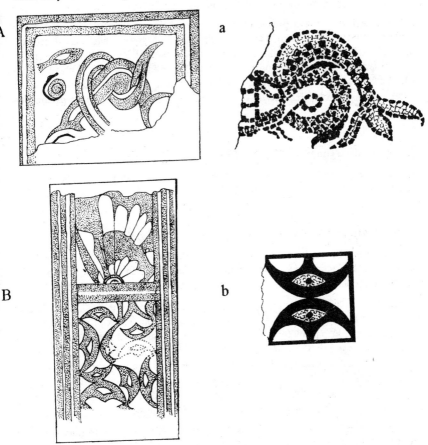

A & B: Maesderwen mosaics, re-drawn from the 1785 representation.

a: Nether end of 'sea monster' & b: Pelta design. Both from a mosaic floor at Withington, Gloucestershire. Drawn from photographs of 1817 engraving.

The 'Pelta' or double-axe motif was used throughout the Roman period on a variety of objects (see the Cerreg Gwynion necklace). It was taken as a symbol of the Amazons, a matriarchal tribe who made the Romans rather edgy.

eighteenth-century depiction, it might have been something like the single monster's nether-end known from Withington, in Gloucestershire. There the *pelta* (double-axe) motif was used as the final band in the overall design of the same floor. At Maesderwen, in the half-size floor of the Cold Room, an elaborated *pelta* was used below what may have been a stepped-fan design like that at the top of the Bucklersbury Pavement (Museum of London).

It is imaginable that a process begun by alterations undertaken in later Roman times, continued by damage due to burial, vegetation growth and animal activity, and culminating in enthusiastic tree-felling, presented the eighteenth century draughtsman with cumulative peculiarities which he had no way of disentangling. At least he has left us with a lively impression of the rooms designed for the sensuous pleasures of that enviable life-style of *otium cum dignitate* so desired by the true Roman.

[Brecon Canal (find) : SO 1387 1985   LR 161   BR

Older records refer to a 'Roman sacrificial knife' found during the digging of the canal in the 1790s. The piece is not Roman.]

Llan-gors (charter evidence) : ?SO 12 NW LR 161   BR

Early mediaeval records indicate that there may have been a villa-estate somewhere in this area. No remains have been found, and nothing gives any indication of what, if any, relationship such an estate might have had with the residence at Maesderwen.

However emphatic a statement of personal taste and standing the actual dwelling of a villa may have been, they were no holiday-homes, but centres of vast agricultural estates, farmed in part by tenants, and using free and slave labour. It was axiomatic of Romanisation that the native population (except the very lowest classes) should adopt the social apparatus and economic systems on which the Empire depended. If not a Roman Gaul, the owner of an estate such as Maesderwen could equally easily have been an Asian mine-director, a retired Dalmatian governor, or a British civil-servant; all would have ordered the estate along the same, imperial lines.

The prosperity of the villa was invested in mixed farming - but farming as known to a Roman world, and therefore far more diverse and cosmopolitan than anything in native tradition. Roots were grown for winter fodder to supplement hay - the turnip coming in with the toga; horse-beans and lentils show that seed was imported; vineyards were planted, and medlars, pears and mulberries introduced. Many of the herbs - dill and fennel, for example - taken for granted by mediaeval and New Age herbalists were first grown in Roman gardens, shaded by the novel walnut tree and the exotic plum. The radical radish and the cabbage, prized for its efficacy the Morning After, arrived in Britain with peas and broccoli, figs and asparagus.

These vegetable wonders, as well as being grown for the villa dining-room, supplied the town markets. The big forts ran their own ranches, and there were also imperial lands; but the villa estates were the bases of the economy of Civilisation. The rustic, the pleb and the barbarian might subsist on half-stewed brisket, gamey horse-meat and curds, but the ranking officers, administrative echelons and literate classes had left all that behind in history. It was the produce of the villas that sustained the Civilisation of the Stomachs. Not fancying butter, which was thrown to the menials, the Romans imported Mediterranean oil into Britain in vast amphorae - the broken sherds of which are such a common find; but native oysters and thyme-honey, several differently treated types of milk, pungent cheeses, mushrooms, nuts and fish were all marketed in the local *vicus* or the nearest large civil settlement (in this case the *vici* outside Brecon Gaer and *BANNIUM*).

The pastures of the villa-estates were not always divided into field-systems; there is evidence that horses and cattle ranged together, as they did on the military *prata*, herded by cowboys and feeding on a mixture of open and wooded land. The small Celtic cattle (*bos longifrons*) were the stock of both Occupier and native, but bone analysis shows that the Romans also imported some of their own, larger breeds, and attempted to up-grade the size of local horses. Roman ox-carts and waggons were extremely efficient, and capable of hauling tremendous loads. Pliny, at the beginning of the second century, thought nothing of sending off by post for a set of marble columns. The hides of these animals were turned into raw-hide or tanned for leather, of which the army used a massive amount, for example in body armour, shields, tents and harness. Wool was an important resource in Britain. There was even a special woollen coat known as 'British', and British woollen horse-rugs were valued along with woolly floor-rugs. Although mutton was not thought much of, the Romans developed an improved sheep with a white fleece - with resounding theological and sartorial consequences - for which much woodland was sacrificed.

Above all there was the production of grain: grain for the administration and grain for the army. Grain was taxed: a levy of up to a half of the yield might be taken by the state. Wheat and barley were the main crops, wheat being so much preferred that barley rations were substituted as a form of punishment. These were often intersown with vetch, and rye was a Roman favourite. Its greater resistance to hard winters gave it an edge over oats, which was relegated to fodder - the expansion of cavalry activities is mirrored in the archaeological record by the expansion of the oat-crop. Rye, however, is very susceptible to spoiling by fungus, in which condition it can produce mass fatal food-poisoning resembling a 'plague' in effect. Granaries in villa and fort were built with ingenious precautions against such mildew, and against rodents: raised off the ground, fumigated and plastered over with sour vinegars.

However over-polished a picture we may have of the villa as a haunt of toga'd poets, it was in reality the centre of vigorous agricultural activity: a place of querns and threshing-rounds; of horse-shoes, whips and nicely balanced sickles; of barns and sheds and labourers and slaves; of overseers, carters and smiths.

Llan-gors Lake : SO 13 26   LR 161   BR

Underwater archaeologists recovered a large Roman brooch during research in the lake in 1991. There are several magnificent examples of this 'Dolphin' type of brooch in the National Museum in Cardiff, some of which come from Ogof yr Esgyrn (q.v.). Underwater archaeology is a young and exciting branch of the science. A research programme to explore the wealth of objects lost or deposited underwater was inaugurated in Ulster in the mid 1990s.

The Lechfaen Cockerel : SO 08 28   LR 160   BR

A find, in the late 1970s, of part of a pipe-clay cockerel caused some excitement. Initially interpreted as a Roman cult object, it was subsequently defrocked and put down to nineteenth century ornamental status. The discussion is not quite over, though...

Brecon Museum   Town Centre   LR 160   BR

The museum is appositely situated where RR 62a passes under the modern town. The building is at the point of a V. To its north, RR 621 passed to the right of the museum (facing the entrance) and on to St. John's Gate. Here it was joined by the link road which connected the highway with the fort, via RR 62a. RR 62a itself passed to the left of the museum entrance and out to the fort between the by-roads to Cradoc and Frenni-fach.

The museum houses three spectacular stone works: Maen y Morwynion (q.v.), the Candidus stone (q.v.) and the Millbrook milestone (q.v.). These are all, in contrasting ways, core pieces. From them, something of the essence of Romanity still emanates - of individual persons, of the skills of literacy and sculpture, and of the sheer mastery of distance.

The finest items from Brecon Fort are in the National Museum collection in Cardiff, but there are many fascinating pieces here, including an evocative display of pottery, spoons and a very nice lamp, set out as they might have been used together. There is much information and a number of smaller personal possessions: beads and dice; a delightful seal-box; brooches, pins and geometric dividers, and a little carved horse's head, which may have belonged to a trooper of the Vettonian cavalry.

Maen y Morwynion   Now in Brecon Museum   LR 160   BR

This weathered and indistinct tombstone used to stand beside the RR 62a, just east of the fort. This section of the road can be seen as a lane running at right angles to the modern farm track, just before it reaches the house at Y Gaer farm. The stone is known to have been found near the fort in the sixteenth century; Camden saw it looming, fretted and slightly sinister, among thin saplings. Even in its present, protective captivity, it is an archetypal dream of an Antiquity.

The last line of the indistinct inscription reads: **CONIUNX EIUS H.S.E.**, and means that the stone was set up by "his wife. He is buried here." Many interpretations have been offered for the lines above, although only a few letters can be identified. The figures, now seemingly withdrawn into the past beyond recall, represent a man and a woman in a formal semi-embrace. This pose was a convention depicting matrimony, not a portrayal of personal affection. An exquisite drawing in the RCAHMW's Brecon Inventory (1986) illustrates as much of the tombstone as can reasonably be reconstructed. It has been dated to AD 75-80, the first years of Brecon Gaer fort. Before its significance was recognised, the relief was thought to represent two women, hence its old, local name, *Maen y Morwynion*, the Maidens' Stone.

Lost Tombstone (RIB 405) : [SO 702 291]   BR

This stone was taken to Brecon Priory before 1684, when it was seen there. It was said to have come from the fort, though this may mean close to, rather than within, the walls. It was a diptych-style monument, of which old drawings exist. It reads: "To the spirits of the departed (and) of Valerius Primus, son of ..., trooper of the cavalry squadron, ..., *optio*; his heir had this set up." (Trans: R.G.Collingwood.)

It was along this part of the road that the burials from the fort and civil settlement at Brecon Gaer (q.v.) were deposited. The road ran among the tombstones, commemorative tablets and buried urns, through a sort of Death City, before entering the commercial outskirts at the north gate of the fort. The Romans indulged in some rather unsettling mortuary practices, which included supplying the corpse with hobnailed boots for the rigours of the journey to the Afterworld. Urns, tanks and depositories for bones and ashes might even be supplied with little culverts down which soothing libations might be poured, and these would stick up above the burial. Perhaps the oddest was their way of keeping cremated remains in a quite transparent glass demijohn.

Route 4 : RR 621 (South) - The Road up to Brecon Gaer from Cardiff

This spinal road runs north up the valleys and over the Brecon Beacons from the middle of the fat, fertile Severnside which Frontinus fought so hard to secure in the early days. At Brecon Gaer, as a spoke joins a hub, it converges with a system of military roads reaching into every part of Wales and the Marches. Its northern section, from Y Gaer to Castell Collen, links these two focal points in central Wales, mid-way between the Irish Sea to the west and Watling Street in the east.

Its southern section started in Cardiff. The Roman courses which can still be seen at the base of the present castle wall date from the last centuries of the Occupation; the earliest fort was immediately to the south, under the most up-market of the capital's shops and watering-holes.

RR 621 ran north through the fort at Caerphilly, and has been verified around Gelligaer (Glamorganshire), where there was a military station with tile and pottery kilns, and what could be a parade-ground. The actual fort (of which there is a splendid model in the National Museum of Wales) is behind St. Cattwg's church, at ST 133 974, on the north-west side of the town centre. The temporary camp lies just beyond it below the pub, and there is a series of practice camps on the heights above Bargoed (ST 135 996).

The re-occupation of Gelligaer stone fort, in the third and fourth centuries, was probably a response, not to the having-been-subdued-and-now-very-Roman Silures, but to the overt intentions of Irish pirates. Raiding the whole west coast of Britain, purloining slaves and saddles, these blood-and-epic Celts presented such a threat that the occupying Romans built massive defences and naval stations against them at Cardiff and Holyhead. Once the Romans had withdrawn, at the end of the fourth century, the Irish did indeed sweep in. They occupied much of north Wales, reaching as far inland as Wroxeter (where they left a Wolf-king and stole St. Patrick), and founded the Irish kingdom of Demetia in modern Dyfed. According to tradition (compounded by some tangled early proto-history, literary and archaeological), the founder of the kingdom of Brycheiniog (modern Breconshire) was one Brychan, aristocratic son of a late fifth-century Irish invader.

Gelligaer and Brecon Gaer both show possible responses to the opening salvoes of these adventures. However the large and elaborate fort at Pen-y-Darren (SO 050 068, Glamorganshire - now under a football pitch near Prince Charles' Hospital), excavated at the beginning of the century, seems to have been in service only from Frontinus' to Hadrian's time. RR 621 runs northwards through Pen-y-Darren and up towards Pontiscill, where it comes into Breconshire.

Vaynor (find) :   **SO 0 1 SW   LR 160   BR/GLamorganshire**

This hoard, found at the end of the Second World War, includes coins of three emperors who all claimed the Imperial purple at the same time - a sort of ancient each-way bet which the gambler was prevented from collecting.

The Emperors in question included Constantine (called the Great) in York and Maxentius (AD 306-12) in Rome. In the end Constantine came out on top, an outcome he attributed directly to the intervention of Jesus Christ in the battle of the Milvian Bridge in 312. After this, Christianity was first declared legal and eventually (324) preferred throughout the Empire. It was Constantine's mother, Helena (David Jones' *'Helen of the Bright Roads'*), after whom the Roman roads are called 'Sarn Helen'. (The fact that mediaeval mythology conflated two Helens does nothing to tarnish the beauty of the concept.)

Bryn Mawr (find) : **SO 1-2 1   LR 161   BR/GL**

Another coin of Constantine the Great was reported from the town, which lies mid-way between RRs 621 and 62a.

The road seems to have gone through the valley, now the Llwyn-on Reservoir, beyond which it possibly met the RR 620 (this is not verified). It is presumed to have run into Brecon much where the modern bridge is now, there to have joined the 62a, running west to Brecon Gaer. It entered the fort through the cemetery area at the end of RR 62a, along what is now a very beautiful (private) farm lane which can be seen through a gateway on the private road up to Gaer farm.

Brecon Gaer Auxiliary Fort : **SO 002 297   LR 160   BR**

Also known as Y Gaer & **Brecon/Aberyscir Roman Fort**

"...and with so great armyes as they had they might doe mighty things." So said Edward Lhuyd of the Romans; and so, at Y Gaer, they did.

Of the Mighty Things, the massive walls and the great stone stumps of watch-towers and magnificent gateways have been left open, and are on view to the public. Perhaps because Y Gaer is in the fields, and not shouldered and overlooked by recent buildings, there is still something alien and remorseless about its heavy stonework and deliberate lines. The fortifications are Scheduled Ancient Monuments, and Cadw have a plan of the actual fort mounted at the entrance. Although there is no written explanation to go with this, an independent guide-book to Y Gaer is available locally. Please note that the farm is private, and does **not** sell any leaflets, booklets etc. While the Scheduled areas (visible, upstanding remains) are open to the public, the surrounding sites, where nothing can be seen on the

MILITARY STATION AT BRECON GAER

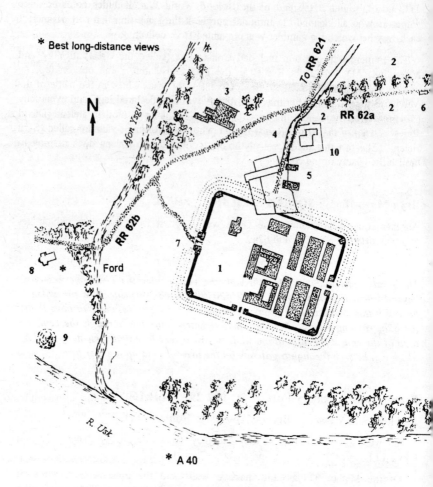

* Best long-distance views

N ↑

Afon Ysgir

To RR 621

RR 62a

RR 62b

Ford

R. Usk

* A 40

1. Fort
2. Cemetery areas
3. *Mansio*
4. *Vicus* areas
5. Commercial Buildings
6. Maen y Morwynion
7. Ceremonial entrance
8. Church
9. *Motte*
10. Modern farm and yards

(Sketch based on maps published by R.E.M. Wheeler, 1929)

ground, are in working farmyards and fields, and there is no right of access.

The first military installation was begun in about AD 75, when the Silures were intractably rebellious, and Frontinus had the task of reducing them to passivity by one means or another. In the event, he tempted them with Roman materialism, and killed them if they didn't fall for it. It proved a very successful strategy, but the necessity for the army to stand-to north of the Severn fat-lands remained, and Y Gaer was re-designed and rebuilt several times in the succeeding centuries.

The earliest station was the type of turf and timber structure which underlies many of the stone-built forts. It has often been suggested that one of the buildings in the central block may have been stabling. Quite recently a block of stables like modern loose-boxes has been excavated at *BURRIUM* (Usk), and has been interpreted as winter quarters for auxiliary cavalry. This discovery makes it possible to see the 'stables' at Y Gaer as nothing more than covered-in horse-lines, perhaps for use only during the campaigning season. The long, thin building opens into an unusual, but not unique, covered 'fore-hall', which has been interpreted as a menage for cavalry practice in the harsh Brecon winters. Experience of the campaigning season in Breconshire suggests that, even if the cavalry were withdrawn during the worst of the winters, there would still have been plenty of occasions for its use. Similar 'fore-halls' are often, but not always, associated with known cavalry barracks; and amongst the troops quartered in Y Gaer was a cohort of Vettonian cavalry, recruited in Spain. The tombstone of a youngster of twenty from this unit was found a mile north of the fort. The inscription does not say how he met his death, or exactly where, but gives his name as Candidus (q.v.).

The wooden *Principia* and *Praetorium* of the earliest fort, and its timber-laced ramparts and watch-towers, were rebuilt in stone by men of *LEG II AVG* during the second century. Controversy stirs over the dating and intentions of this rebuilding. It may be that the fort was now intended to serve only half its original complement. Alternatively, having been condensed during one of the Wall-building phases, it may have been purposefully re-designed on a reduced scale to serve either as a base for troops redundant once the Wall was up, or as a garrison fortress for renewed activities amongst the resurgent Celts. In 1993 the discovery, just outside the south-west corner, of over sixty sherds of a predominantly Antonine date indicates considerable activity in the mid-second century; this may have been related to the re-building of the fort. Whatever the reason, while the eight barracks behind them were left as wooden-plank units, the central block of *Principia*, *Praetorium*, and the heavily buttressed granary was rebuilt in stone. The *Praetorium* at Y Gaer - the living quarters of the Commanding Officer - was equipped with an additional kitchen, perhaps at the behest of one particular commander with gastronomic interests. It would be in the *Praetorium* that tactics, strategies and, no doubt, imperial politics would be discussed over sweet Italian wines, Greek olives, and flaky little dormouse rolls. The *Principia*, on the other hand, was the soul-house of the garrison. Here the tall, silver eagles and honours, the statues of emperors, and altars to the gods hallowed the internal shrine. Here the sacrifices were made, and auguries read below the shrill squealing of pipes through which no inauspicious sound might penetrate; here the courts martial sat, the weird horn *bucina* at hand to raise the adrenalin at the moment of an execution.

The original bath-building seems to have lain under the modern barn just outside the North Gate. At some point it, too, was rebuilt, this time in the empty half of the interior of the fort. Compared with the elaborate structure at Castell Collen, and as military baths generally go, Y Gaer's bath-house is a poor wee thing; and this has been taken as a reflection of the inferior social standing of the auxiliary troops. The bath-block is set at a marked angle to the other buildings (oddly enough, the *Praetorium* is also slightly mis-aligned, giving cause for much speculation among scholars).

More conventionally, great double-arched gates, and guard-lodges with painted interiors, gave passage through the new, stone-faced walls. It is the footings of these entrances, the pivot-holes of the gates themselves, and the stumps of dressed architectural features which are still there to be seen: massive stone remnants set in powerful stone banks between the foundations of the guard-rooms. [See the photograph of the South Gate, p. 40.] Through the Ceremonial Gate in the west wall would ride the renowned and the favoured, to the blaring of the martial trumpets and horns, the clashing of cymbals and the rhythmic screech of nailed boots on stone.

There is a considerable stretch of rampart wall, coursed and upstanding to an impressive height on the north side. The heavier, cruder stone of the ultimate repair-work (probably fourth century) is quite noticeable in the spill and rubble around the north-east quarter. After the sod-dulled ridges and rabbit-run banks of other remains in the county, there is something stark, even shocking, about the exposed stone-work of Y Gaer.

Y Gaer was not just the fort, although that is all that is now visible. Aerial photography has shown up a **Practice camp** at SO 000 298, just beside the unmade modern road to the church; and under the modern yard of Y Gaer Farm RR 621 (north) was flanked by commercial and service booths: blacksmiths, tanners, shops, with living quarters behind. One of these, at least, was built within fifty years of the fort's inception - a coin of Trajan was found in mint condition between floor levels of what may have been an official smithy. Iron-working was, of course, a priority occupation: the Empire's need for metal ores was one of the principal reasons for the invasion, and accounts in some measure for the ferocity and thoroughness of the Conquest, particularly in Wales.

The foundations of these commercial buildings extend for some distance along the road, and are now partly covered by the modern farm lane which leads up from the Aberyscir side-road. These extra-mural buildings, and the cemetery to the east, where *Maen y Morwynion* (q.v.) once loomed, together suggest that there was a

Above: Building Stone
in Tretower House
gate-pier (RIB 402).

Right: Brecon Gaer,
South Gate.

Above: RR 622, north of Coelbren.

Left: Today's by-road covering RR 623, just south of Caerau.

considerable associated population, attracted by the presence of the garrison.

Diagonally to the north-west of the fort, and perched on the brink of the steep slope down into the cwm, there was a Residence (*mansio*) of some magnitude, probably for use by visiting high-ranking officials and by the Imperial Post. The intaglios of four rings were recovered from here, and are permanently exhibited in the National Museum of Wales. One of them, a glass piece showing a naked and helmeted Ulysses with his dog, is particularly vivid and suitably martial. The Romans kept a wary eye on Fortuna, and these amazing little engravings were not seals but mascots.

Maen y Morwynion was set up by somebody's widow; evidently Y Gaer was a post to which families accompanied senior military and administrative officers. Certainly, it is likely that the Officer in Command would have had some domestic life. Eight bone draughtsmen, some dice, a spindle-whorl and a clutch of bluey-green beads give us brief glimpses of life off duty. Another intaglio, a carnelian showing Drama masked as Comedy and holding the companion-face of Tragedy, suggests that all sense of entertainment was not annihilated by horse-gear and ballista-points.

Out to the west, along RR 62b, lay Llanio, also an auxiliary fort, and guardian of the gold-mines. From there comes a little yew-wood carving of a woman's head. It

 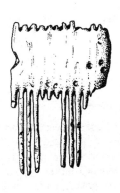

a.

b.

a: Severe head of the Llanio matron (drawn from photographs).

b: Antler comb from Ogof yr Esgyrn (re-drawn after W.F.Grimes).

Pliny, in one of his ubiquitous condolence letters, considers the mounting of a public Gladiatorial Combat a fitting tribute to the lately deceased wife of one of his acquaintances. In the light of this, one can only regard the severity of the Llanio head with some awe.

may have been a token image deposited at a shrine as a form of the sympathetic magic crossed with faith-healing to which the Romans were much given. [An arm, not necessarily belonging to the same piece, turned up independently.] Alternatively, it may have decorated the end of a wand or even a walking-stick. The hair-style is apparently that Roman coiffure, unhelpfully known as 'melon', which appears on sculptures and wall-paintings in Italy in the second and early third centuries. Although it certainly depicts a Roman woman, the precise centre of the forehead hairline is dressed in a very Celtic shape. This, together with the way in which the strands of hair are shown, has been taken to indicate that the carving was made by a British craftsman. Since Y Gaer is half-way between Llanio and both the legionary fort at *ISCA* (Caerleon) and the civilian township at *VENTA* (Caerwent), many a formidable Roman matron must have travelled along RR 621, perhaps resting in the Residence.

There is a considerable dissonance between the custodial 'melon' and the matted locks that reputedly wore away the teeth of the comb found in Ogof yr Esgyrn (q.v.).

*

Route 5 : RR 622 - The Road up to Brecon Gaer from NIDUM (Neath)

Mynydd y Drum : SN 826 112   LR 160   BR

(Environmental Site)

As a technique, 'pollen analysis' sounds boring. On the page, it looks very boring - an expanse of dots and Xs on lines, or a series of little black rectangles. In fact, a pollen diagram is thrilling. This is what happens: The buried pollen collected from a site is examined under a microscope, and it is possible to tell from what species most of the grains derive. On an archaeological site, where the soil is layered - the oldest at the bottom - the grains from each level are kept separate. Then a diagram is made, showing how many of which species occurred in which successive layer. Still boring. But once the eye is accustomed to 'reading' these diagrams, a whole lost landscape comes back out of the past with its great trees, its bushes and grazing grounds, its soggy reed patches, clusters of wild flowers, and intimate, mossy hollows. This is not imagining an ancient landscape - this is seeing it.

The diagram made from analysing the pollen from peat in a depression in the bog up on Mynydd y Drum shows that by the time the Romans came into the area, the uplands were largely open. The natural forest had already been cleared. Then, during the Occupation, considerably more sedges and grasses appear, and there is an incidence of a cereal from crops growing somewhere in the area.

The Romans made colossal demands on the land. The Administration, as well as the army, ate. The increase in the demand for provisions was substantial. Not only did the occupiers and their animals present an actual and instant rise in the population; their attitude to food was necessarily different. Food had to be predictably regular. If the legions starved, the Empire fell. There was no room for dependency on a wayward zephyr.

The paired ovens built against the ramparts of forts provided that most basic item: bread. The legionaries (voluntary career-soldiers and Roman citizens) ate loaves made from wheat or rye. Dispiritingly, these, like their forts, were rectangular; like their bricks, they were stamped *LEG II AVG*. To meet this huge demand for cereals, there was an extension of arable farming into the woodlands not cleared by the existing Iron Age population. It used to be said that the legions did not eat meat, but re-interpretation of the evidence has dispelled this uplifting theory. It seems that the catering corps were occasionally reduced to serving up flesh which provoked even campaigning infantry to temporary vegetarianism.

The Roman forts, villas and larger settlements were set in fertile river-valleys; while their more efficient farming techniques would have increased the productivity of the surrounding area, there was still a need for further clearance. The opening of sheep-walks - wool from sheep was more important than their mutton - added to the felling of timber for military and civil buildings. However water-wheels (such as that at Dolau-Cothi), bridges, and quays for water-borne transport were all made of wood, as well as military machines like catapults, rams and the handles of small-arms; charcoal was used in vast quantities for metal-working and pottery firing. The evidence for re-planting is scant but, intriguingly, not totally absent.

One of the effects of clearance by this foreign host, which shows up evocatively in the pollen diagrams, was a colour-change. It was the Romans (red-tunic'd as they were) who brought, with their imported victuals, the seeds of the scarlet pimpernel and the brilliant poppy to the new, open fields. Indeed, there is some evidence that whole fields of poppies may have been grown for their seed. Like an ancient battle-honour, their brilliance has remained on British land ever since.

When the Empire collapsed it left a desolation made not only by its absence, but by the absence of the native culture which the Occupation had largely destroyed. Into this social and physical wilderness, the trees came again. Saplings of birch and hazel crept over road and ranch, and cracked apart the stone-work of the Second Legion Augustus. Little Xs on a line...

Coelbren Fort :   SN 859 107   LR 160   GL/BR

Fields now shroud the ramparts of an important wooden fort which stood here above the meeting of two streams, and at the junction of five Roman roads. The modern by-road approximately skirts the north and east banks. These defences still have some presence; entirely grassed over, but easily seen, they surround a domed area grazed by cattle and sheep. The land belongs to the big farm across the road to the east, down the hedged lane and over the stream-bridge. Permission to walk the ramparts should be sought there.

Coelbren is unusual in that, although it was rebuilt like most forts, it was rebuilt in wood, not stone.   This is not unique, but it is rare.   At the beginning of this century, trenches were excavated across small sections of the fort area.   They revealed that the first phase of the surrounding rampart was founded on cobbles and brushwood, some of which was coarse heather, preserved in the peaty soil.   The excavation report makes particular mention of the noxious stench released by marsh-gas when this ancient wood was laid open to the air. Oak planks and barked timbers were used to lace the clay and turf banks, a method of defence structure found in several other ramparts, such as Castell Collen (RA), *LAVOBRINTA* (Forden Gaer, Montgomeryshire) and *BRAVONIUM* (Leintwardine, Herefordshire). Outside the ramparts, a five-metre berm separated them from the double ditches, and wooden watch-towers crowned each corner of the fort.

Inside, the barracks, too, were wooden units with the sills or footings made of sleeper-type oak beams. There were two levels here, the later using wood again, but possibly employing clay, stone or wattle and daub in addition. Some curious stakes about a foot long, found on the west side, may have been tent-pegs, but equally may have been a peculiarly beastly defensive device upon which the feet of horses and men became impaled.

Datable pottery from Frontinus' and Agricola's governorships, and cooking pots from Hadrian's or Antoninus' reigns, show when Coelbren was occupied - probably by a thousand infantry or half that number of auxiliary cavalry. It has been suggested that the Romans demolished the fort themselves as soon as it ceased to be functional.

Quite recently the beginning of one of the roads was seen when the area was being drained. There are tales of previous generations piling up the remnants from the ramparts, and carrying them away to re-use - a common archaeologist's nightmare.

The finds from Coelbren, including some wood, are on permanent display in Swansea Museum, as the site is properly a few yards into today's Glamorganshire.

Coelbren is pre-eminently a cross-roads station of strategic significance. To it, RR 622 came up from the sea at Neath, through the fort environs, and on north-eastwards to Brecon Gaer. RRX 84 left for the north-west and Llandovery; RRX 83 ran due west in the direction of the modern town of Coelbren, and its fellow, RRX 86, eastwards to Pen-y-Darren (GL). The gate-gaps, and the causeways where the fort roads emerged on to these highways, were visible in 1907 when the trenches were excavated, but they have been ploughed out in this century.

RRX 84 went up north-west to Llandovery fort (ALABVM) through the limestone gorges and punitive uplands of the Black Mountain Forest. From these the fractious hillsmen had swept down to ravage the Conquest camps. The limestone-forming epoch came after Lapworth's 'Ordovician' period, and before the fierce desert world which created the Old Red Sandstone. In 1835, Murchison named it in the hillsmen's honour: the Silurian, he called it.

Ogof yr Esgyrn : SN 8378 1604   LR 160   BR

Called **The Bone Cave**; part of Dan yr Ogof Showcave tourist complex.

This is a curious and macabre site, a world apart from the mosaic'd villa or the precise, verandah'd *Praetorium*. In this low, wide cave, high in the grey limestone, extinct carnivores made lairs in the Ice Ages, and remote cattle-rangers buried their dead in the Bronze Age. What was done here during the Roman Occupation is less clear. A word of warning: The official guide-book to the caves emphasises the older prehistoric finds. As many children romp gleefully through the dinosaurs, and on to enjoy the sabre-tooth tiger and the scarlet-kilted Roman soldier, the more appalling things which seem to have happened in Ogof yr Esgyrn are, rightly, omitted. They are not omitted in the following account.

Today the cave is presented (with life-size models, and audio and lighting effects) as a combined demonstration of prehistoric periods and the techniques of modern excavation. Nearest to the entrance is a model of a Roman legionary of *LEG II AVG*, complete with replica weapons, Eagle, tools and pottery. He wears mail and looks blandly uninvolved. He is here because the remains of no fewer than forty individuals were interred in the cave during the Occupation. As well as bodies, a variety of personal effects were deposited or left here, in the dark, with a number of food-bones, sherds of pottery, and some coins. The burials and fine objects have been dated to the second century, although the cave was occupied again fleetingly in the fourth century.

One of the magnificent brooches from the cave. Redrawn after W.F.Grimes.

The earlier finds are an ambiguous collection. Of the seven bronze brooches some, especially the two 'dolphin' brooches, are unusually large and fine. These, together with seal-box, bracelet, ring and the metal end-casing (terminal) of a leather strap are Roman objects, not the possessions of a Celtic cave-dweller. One of the smaller brooches is of a Spanish penannular 'omega' type; the Vettonian cavalry at Brecon Gaer and the Asturian cohort at Llanio were both Spanish. All of these, along with fragments of Roman glass, Samian pottery and a coin of Vespasian stuck to some shreds of flax fibre from its original linen purse, could be explained as booty from an ambush.

However, at the back of the area now showing figures of archaeologists at work, the bodies of some twelve persons, male and female, were buried in a loose, sandy area. In the first two centuries the Romans cremated their dead in defined places of defined places of burial. They did not inter them beside the camp-fire.

It is possible that these are the remains of the party of an officer or civil servant travelling, perhaps with his family, from one posting to another. Massacred after a hold-up, were their corpses then buried, by native hillsmen, in the native, Iron Age manner? Among the finds from the second century levels in the cave were some needles, a bodkin and elegant pins made of animal bone. There was also part of a comb worked from antler, the teeth of which are described as being scored as if by "combing long and tangled hair". [See p. 42.] All of this could indicate that this cave, like others in Wales, was used by Celts as a dwelling. It is just possible that they might have lightly buried the cadavers of the ambushed enemy just behind the hearth...

As well as some ox and pig bones there were a great number of sheep remains (little creatures, under two feet high). Of these, an abnormal number were lamb-bones. This indicates a feast - even that beloved scenario: the Ritual Feast. This hypothesis becomes sinister in the light of the remaining discoveries. In the centre of the cave were the skeletal remains of another four adults and of eight children between six and eight years old, mostly seven to eight. The jaw-bones of some of them were noticeably well developed; these children were not physically disadvantaged, nor were they perennially unhealthy. Furthermore, allowing for the differential movement of the long and 'plate-shaped' bones by animals, water and other natural disturbances, and all such archaeological considerations, there is still an undue proportion of skull material.

Naturally, all sorts of interpretations have been offered to explain, or explain away, these disturbing remains. There is no known 'natural cause' which selects healthy seven-year-olds. Just 'robbers' is really insufficient - some forty individuals were represented in the burials, and some of them only by their skulls. Head-hunting is a colourfully advertised Iron Age Celtic activity. Should it be considered in a context of seven-year-old children, it would become singularly unheroic.

When the cave was re-occupied in the fourth century, these terrible relics seem to have been disregarded. Fires were lit over the graves, and cinders and sherds dropped down among the buried bones. How much could be seen by the uncertain light of flaring torches and sputtering cooking-hearths?

In the museum beneath the Showcave complex, there is an exhibition of very well made replicas of the finds (the originals are in the National Museum of Wales), accompanied by some extremely interesting information on the Roman presence in South Wales. This is an excellent display, ironically overseen by a life-size standard-bearer in full wolf-pelt insignia.

Back on the red sandstone, RR 622 shows up clearly where it leaves Coelbren fort through its east gateway. The wide range of the agger is quite distinct, running under the modern road and down to the stream. The road's line through the fields

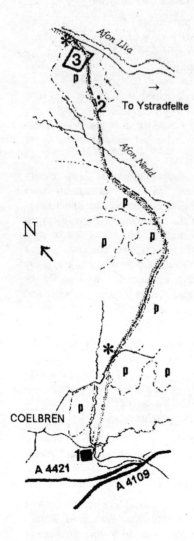

1. Coelbren Fort
2. Dervacus Stone
3 . Ystradfellte Marching Camp
p   Forestry plantations

*   Car parking for walk

behind the farm is, in places, spectacularly present, and can be seen from a variety of viewpoints on the surrounding slopes. It is a good beginning to a major road, long stretches of which can be ridden, and more walked, for much of its way to Brecon Gaer. It is marked on the map as Sarn Helen. Something of the implacable grandeur which, even today, rings in the very words 'the Roman Roads', still drifts about this strait and ancient highway.

From the gate at SN 879 116 the military road strikes out north-east into the hills, bleak and uncompromising among the high winds. [See the photograph on page 41.] What nailed boots rang on the large, flat stones, coloured like dried blood, which lie silent in the ruts and pools of the track?

Ystradfellte (find) :

SN 9 1 SW   LR 160   BR

A gold coin of Vespasian, Emperor throughout Frontinus' period of service in Britain, was found here in the eighteenth century. Vespasian commanded *LEG II AVG* during the Conquest, and it is thought that his especial brief was to locate and secure the mining areas for which the west of Britain was famed. To this end, *II AVG* spent the early years in Somerset and the West Country before moving up to Severnside.

At c.SN 915 150 there is another magnificent stretch of RR 622, rising up from the crossing of the Nedd, and running across high moorland towards Plas-y-gors plantation. The soil under the road here is of a type formed in the same sort of upland moor which the road crosses today. It must have looked much the same to a young

Candidus or an exhausted legionary of Peregrinus' century as it does to us now.
But it would have smelled and sounded different. Nearby, at Ystradfellte, there is
pollen evidence for oakwoods at the time of the Conquest, such as were felled for
the ramparts of Coelbren. Where today the commercial plantations have created a
hushed, coniferous desert, the woods standing in Roman times would have been
loud with birdsong, crackling with the nervous life of predator and prey. Today one
can grin at scatty fox-cubs rolling on their backs in the spring sun up here; in
Roman times wolf, bear and the wicked wild boar threatened from the odorous
leaf-mould.

Dervacus son of Justus

he lies here : at SN 918 157   LR 160   BR

ECM 73, known and marked as Maen Madog Stone

The starkest of all the inscribed stones in Wales, this bleak memorial was raised
right on the edge of the Roman road, in Roman funerary tradition. It is ill-writ, some
of the letters back to front, and the As upside down. Unusually, it has no parallel
Ogham transcription, as do other inscribed stones in the area. It has been suggested
that it may commemorate one who farmed a relic villa estate in the valley to the
west, in that post-Roman tradition which lingered on into the earliest Middle Ages.

When it was investigated in 1940, it was seen that the stone had already fallen and
been re-erected, not in its original position, but on the very edge of the Roman road.
Some feet back from it, a large square pit was uncovered, which may have been the
grave of Dervacus himself. RR 622 actually lies under the rough moorland, a few
feet to the south-east of the modern track, sixteen feet wide and metalled with river
stones rammed into a clay foundation. It was into this secure footing that the stone
was re-erected after its first collapse. Initially it would have stood back from the
Roman road, at the grave (today's aspect is more or less the same, displaced a few
feet).

The relationship of Dervacus' burial to the road is interesting, but not unique.
Whether its relationship to Ystradfellte Camp is co-incidental, is unknown.

Ystradfellte Marching Camp : SN 924 164   LR 160   BR

Also known as Plas-y-Gors

This camp lurks deep in the gloom of regimented spruces, a quarter of a mile north-
east along the Roman road from Dervacus' stone. It is not easy to see. Where the
south side crosses the (forestry) track, there is a faint rise in the surface of the track,
and a thin brake between the trees along the south rampart. The camp is a Scheduled
Monument, and the line of the defences was left unplanted; however the trees are
now mature, and their long, sweeping branches quite obscure any sense of the

presence of the fort. Recently a new track has nicked through the north-east corner, further on near where the established track arrives at the road. There is a clavicular entrance on the west side, but no legitimate (or comfortable) way of reaching it. The modern track enters through the south, possibly where the gateway was, crosses the camp diagonally, and emerges at a possible east gateway.

When the trees are harvested, this should be a spectacular site, with the military road stretching out across the hills in both directions; but until then much depends on the eye of faith.

RR 622 continues along the modern side-road for a short stretch and then strikes out again as a north-easterly track running behind Maen Llia, the gigantic standing stone. A tough walk, the Roman road curves into the fold of the west side of the mountain, about two thirds of the way up. The present road descends precipitously into the Senni valley, at an impossible gradient for ox-waggons. From the valley floor the Roman route can easily be seen, high above on the line of the footpath.

Nant Cwm-du : SN 942 215   LR 160   BR

A rim-sherd of late second or early third century Samian ware was found in the deep stream-cut side-valley. The elegant vessel of which it is the remnant was probably made far off in eastern Gaul - only to fall off the back of a Silurian porter or a captive-drawn draft waggon on that grim, shelterless road....

A short distance from Nant Cwm-du, the RR 622 crabs sideways across the hillside to lower ground, and emerges on to a quiet side-road a few yards from Forest Lodge. From the gate here (c.SN 9620 2425) the line of the road can be seen and walked south-west back towards Cwm-du. From this gate, in the opposite direction, the road goes forward, north-east towards Brecon Gaer, as a stretch of by-road running straight to the A 4215.

For anyone who has difficulty walking, but would enjoy actually being on a stretch of Roman road, this is an ideal place. Both the road and the track are quiet and absolutely level, and there is space to park a car.

The Road at Mynydd Illtyd SN 977 268
LR 160 BR

This is an amenable, easily reached and wonderfully located stretch of road on Mynydd Illtyd. Nearby, the Libanus Mountain Centre has some magnificent photographs of the agger, and an excellent information board.

The Roman road runs athwart the unfenced modern road as a wide ridge among the gorse bushes. It passes behind the farm and on beside the wall in the fields bordering the north east of the open moor. Illtyd, for whom the hillside is named, was one of the most important of the earliest Christian 'saints' working in post-Roman Britain. Sites associated with him reach up through Breconshire, and north as far as the Merionethshire coast. Some Roman roads were deliberately kept up for a while after the withdrawal of the legions, and local communities continued to use them for far longer, even if any repair-work was on an ad hoc basis. The burial of Dervacus by the roadside, and the mantle of Illtyd cast over the hill, are markers of the significance the roads still had in the spread of the early Celtic churches.

From Mynydd Illtyd, the line of RR 622 to Brecon Gaer is lost. There is no sign of where it crosses the A 40 to reach the South Gate of the fort; it may have linked up with the 62b to enter at the West Gate.

*

Route 6 : RR 62b - The Gold-Road from Brecon Gaer to Llandovery and the West

RR 62b, to the forts at Llandovery (ALABUM) and Llanio (BREMIA), leaves Brecon Gaer by the ceremonial West Gate. The fact that the road was repaired some time between AD 258 and 270 (the reigns of the 'Gallic' Emperors Posthumus and Victorinus) indicates that Brecon Gaer was of some military, and presumably commercial, significance at the very time when the villa baths were built as Maesderwen. It is reasonable to imagine it as carrying civilian as well as military traffic: luxury goods as well as replacement mail; harps and kythera as well as bugles.

The road seems to have curved to the right just outside the fort gate, joined the by-pass to the north of the fort, and then run sideways down the steep hill below the walls. It forded the river immediately below Aberyscir church; the graveyard overlies it. [See sketch map, Brecon Gaer, RR 621.] It was, of course, along the roadside approaches to the forts that the cadavers of the beheaded, crucified and otherwise mutilated were exposed for the edification of all.

Aberyscir Practice Camp : SO 000 298   LR 160   BR

Aerial photography has revealed a practice camp right in the corner of the field where the unmade road turns off south to the church. Not visible from ground level, it is the usual small size of western practice camps. These could be built and demolished in a day - which must have been a bit depressing.

From here on most of 62b's westward course is unproven, but taken to underlie the A 40 to Trecastell.

Defynnog (find): SN 90-95 25-30   LR 160   BR

A hoard, which included a coin showing the head of the wife of Philip the Arab (AD 244-9), was ploughed up in the parish in 1758. Philip's times were turbulent, and the owner never returned...

Trecastell : SN 88 29   LR 160   BR

Rumours of coins found in a garden across from the castle have added to the feeling that there may have been a Roman station here. If there was, scholarly proddings have so far failed to locate it.

Lost Milestone : ?SN 87/8 28/9   LR 160   BR

RIB 2260

When the turnpike road to Llandovery was being made in 1769, a milestone was found two feet down in the ground 'near' the Heath Cock Inn. It was inscribed on both sides (a common feature of milestones). The first, lengthy dedication is to the Emperor and Lord Postumus (AD 260-69): **IMP DO N MAR CASSIA/NO LATINIO/POSTUMO/PIO FEL AVG**. The second dedication is a curt little effort to Postumus' successor, Victorinus (269-71). Both these emperors reigned over the 'Gallic' sub-empire which emerged in the north.

RRX 82e is thought to have diverged from RR 62b at c.SO 873 292 and run south west, perhaps towards the villa site at Llys Brychan (CarMarthen), near Llandeilo. If it did, it would have run past Arhosfa Marching Camp (SN 803 263 CM), otherwise totally isolated.

Maesgwyn : SN 86 30   LR 160   BR

In the middle of the last century, a silver coin of Maximus ('Thrax'), AD 235-8, was found well to the north of the line of the road.

Just west of Trecastle, Ordnance Survey marks as Roman a long, straight stretch of by-road and track. In fact, RCAHMW has shown this to be a turnpike road, and excavation of sections of it has revealed no Roman construction. However, as the Roman road does run along a parallel line of terrace a few yards uphill (north) of the track,. the impressive walk from SN 868 292 to the camps at Y Pigwn is Virtual Reality. There is space to park a car at the end of the metalled road before crossing the moor to Y Pigwn. The Roman sites are a mile and a half further on. The track is very exposed, and can be bitterly cold: windswept and awesome. Perversely, in summer, when the remains are obscured by knee-clutching growth, the upland views are brilliant with larks, buzzards and wild horses.

Y Pigwn : SN 827 312   LR 160   BR/CM

Also known as **Cwm y Cadno**

There is a group of remains here, consisting of a fortlet and a practice camp (which are in fact just in Carmarthenshire), and two huge marching camps which are just in Breconshire. They are set at the brink of the high land before the road plunges down into the Tywy valley where, at Llandovery, a fort guarded the meeting of many waters.

The second marching camp (2 on the sketch map; 26 acres) is built largely inside the first (1; 37.5 acres), but is differently oriented. It is not difficult to follow the outline of this second, smaller camp among the clumps and sheep trails. The best place to pick up the banks of both is by leaving the track and walking a few yards directly uphill to the nearest end of the quarry mounds. These have demolished the south-east side of both camps, but here the south corner of the inner one is an

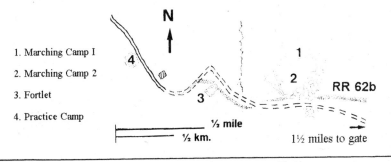

1. Marching Camp I
2. Marching Camp 2
3. Fortlet
4. Practice Camp

N

½ mile
½ km.

RR 62b

1½ miles to gate

excellent point from which to track both sets of ramparts. They appear as low banks or ridges in the heather, bracken and juncus grass, with the corners of the inner camp quite visible, and the outer ones traceable when the vegetation is low. The in-turned clavicular entrances show up as uneven ridges curving in from the entrance gaps, and the ditches outside the ramparts still survive as lines of lying water and soggy strips with reeds growing in ragged patches.

The marching camps were a feature of the Conquest - campaigning camps. It was from such defences that men made marvellous by the pelts of bear and wolf raised the Eagles to steady the foot formations; from behind such defences that the Vettonians and Asturians raced out along the flanks of the infantry when the torc'd and white-maned British came howling across the hills.

Both the camps at Y Pigwn are early - built, perhaps, as part of the initial Conquest. The actual road was constructed and metalled after the camps had ceased to be significant. It is the fortlet, slightly further on at SN 823 310, which guarded the road (3 on the sketch map). It has a single entrance on its north-east side, which would have fronted RR 62b, here running just to the south of the modern/turnpike track. It is, however, difficult to appreciate as the remains of a *motte* confuse the lines, and the Roman structure was very small, especially by comparison with the vast early marching camps. It is most easily seen from a little distance. Further on still, in the fields beyond Hafod Fawr, was a small practice camp at SN 814 313 (4; ploughed out), which may have been associated with the garrison in the fortlet, or with the fort at Llandovery, three or four miles on down the Roman road.

Beyond Y Pigwn, RR 62b crossed the Tywy at Llandovery (ALABUM) and went on through Pumsaint, which guarded the Dolau Cothi gold-mines, to Llanio (BREMIA). At some point in its history BREMIA was garrisoned by the Second cohort of the Asturian cavalry. This troop, like the Vettonians at Brecon Gaer, was raised in north west Spain.

*

The mines of Dolau Cothi (SN 668 404, Carmarthenshire) are owned by the National Trust and presented as an outdoor museum of the history of gold-mining. The extensive Roman workings are open to the public, with very detailed display boards and a wealth of information. It was to these mines that prisoners and criminals were brought along the grim road through Y Pigwn.

'Pliny to the Emperor Trajan: The sentence ... whereby Archippus had been condemned to the mines for forgery ...' [Letter 58]. What terrible justice, to put the keen eyesight and delicate hands of an Archippus to punishment in those dark, coffin-shaped galleries in the dripping rock.

Route 7 : RR 621 (North) - The Road from Brecon Gaer to Castell Collen

Candidus Stone Site :   SO 00 32   LR 160   BR

RIB 403 (Now in Brecon Museum)

The broken inscription to young Candidus was found in a field below the farm of Battle Fawr, north of the village of Battle, and well to the side of both RR 621 and the approach road to Brecon Gaer, RR 62a. This funerary inscription was probably moved from its original site in the fort cemetery as a curiosity, rather than taken for building. It was found in the field in 1877, and is a beautiful piece of inscription, sharp and precise on icily smooth stone.

The letters in the extant half read **DIS.M / CAND / NI.FILI / HISP.VETT / CLEM.DOM / AN.XX.STIP.III.** This, being expanded and interpreted, means: "To the Spirits of the Departed (and) of Candidus, son of ....nus, trooper of the Cavalry Regiment of Vettonian Spaniards, Roman citizens, of the troop of Clemens, from ....; aged 20, of 3 years' service" (Trans. R.G.Collingwood). The wording dates the inscription to the late first or early second century. In AD 103 LEG.II.AVG are known to have been in command of the Vettonians, although where the troop was at that specific date is not mentioned. Perhaps at Brecon Gaer.

Unlike most auxiliary troops, the Vettonian cavalry were all Roman citizens: a regimental honour won on the field. The cavalry of the Conquest were not hand-to-hand or shock troops - those developed later with the adoption of the stirrup from the East and, eventually, the use of heavy armour for horse and rider, which produced that equine version of the tank, the *cataphract*. Candidus' peers were scouts, outriders on the flanks of the infantry, and vengeance-posses who pursued and slaughtered survivors fleeing the field. Their style of riding is shown quite clearly on contemporary tombstones: the feet hanging free and well below the pony's belly, and the loose saddle-cloth with no supporting pommel or cantle.

Most of these troopers rode small pony-stallions, and struck over-arm and downwards at the enemy; the under-arm horizontal thrust in the mediaeval manner would have been impossible from a stirrup-less saddle-pad. It has been suggested that one of the buildings in Brecon Gaer fort may have been covered horse-lines. If it was, it could not have sheltered more than the mounts which every infantry legion had for reconnaissance and despatch riding. If, however, the fort was occupied either entirely or in part by cavalry, the covered lines must surely have been reserved for ranking officers' horses. These seem to have been rather larger and showier. A handle ending in a carved horse's head, which was found at Y Gaer, resembles a northern, stocky pony type far more closely than the flashy Mediterranean horse-flesh which is shown on important sculptural pieces. It is known that the Romans brought horses with them, as well as taking over the mounts

Riding down the Fractious Hillsmen...

Left: RUFUS SITA, trooper of the 6th Cohort, Thracians. Aged 40, he survived 22 years in the cavalry. From a tombstone found near Ermine Street, now in Gloucester City Museum. The Thracians took part in the Claudian Conquest, and were at one stage garrisoned in the early auxiliary fortress at Kingsholm, just outside Gloucester.

Right: Part of a broken and very eroded tombstone from Bath, the only monument in the area erected in memory of a Vettonian trooper. A Vettonian cohort was stationed at Brecon Gaer.

Drawn from photographs.

of the defeated Celts, and that they attempted to breed bigger horses than those available locally. All this suggests that there may have been a distinction between the rapid, tough, manoeuvrable pony used by the trooper of the Conquest, and the martial horse ridden by officers - a difference reflected in carvings and sculpture.

The fragments of the bronze parade helmet and the bronze brooches; the rings and white-metalled links for sections of leather horse-harness; the bits and the cheek-piece pendant which once shone and jangled here: these are now still, silent in the museum cases of Brecon and Cardiff. They were the stuff of young Candidus' life, and the accoutrements of death - not only of the desperate, bitter Celts, but perhaps of Candidus, too.

The superb accuracy of the lettering on this young Spaniard's tomb is a reminder that however sublime and romantically antique the ruins of the forts may be, they are but ruins; in their time, in this place, they must have been terrifying.

Route 7

RR 621, coming north from the coast through Gelligaer to Castell Collen, crossed the Usk at Brecon. It used to be visible on the side of the hill as part of the lane running up to Pen-y-Crug and on towards the Cradoc-Upper Chapel junction, but it can no longer be seen. It was here, at SO 035 311, that it would have been joined by RR 62a from Brecon Gaer. Its course is taken as the line of B 4520 as far as Castle Madoc, where it ran due north, east of the modern road, up to the high ground.

Up here it appears as a hollow-way (LR 147, RA), and from SO 028 410 to SO 023 419 it has been verified as following the footpath from Twyn-y-post north north-west for over half a mile. Its line down to Builth Wells is unproven.

Builth Wells : SO 04 51   LR 147   RA

Whilst it is felt that there ought to be a fort here at the crossing of the Wye, it has not yet been hunted down. There are indications of earthworks of a suitable mien around the Norman castle, and rumours of coins found just south of the bridge.

Colwyn Castle : SO 108 540   LR 148   RA

The Case of Scholarly Proddings Vindicated: a considerable number of Roman sherds turned up near a *motte* not far from Castell Colwyn, where a fort had long been hoped for. The pottery has been dated to the turn of the first century, when the Conquest was largely complete, and the Occupation settling in. A link road, RRX 82, Builth Wells to Clyro, is thought to have passed very close to the site.

The military road, RR 623 (north) from Penmincae, joins the 621 north of Lower Gaufron (SO 040 570). While this cannot be seen on the ground, there is a lay-by very close to it, on the west side of the A 483 at SO 055 570. This commands a magnificent view of the topography through which RRs 623 and 621, and RRXs 79a and 58 find their way. It is worth stopping here with the map to watch for the ghost-geography under the cloud-shadows.

Howey :   SO 042 588   LR 147   RA

A ruined, four-foot wall here is considered by Ordnance Survey to be a mill-pond. In other indices it has appeared as a Roman structure.

Llanfawr Quarry (find): SO 063 616   LR 147   RA

Llandrindod

Some pottery sherds were found in the quarry early in this century.

Cae Bach Chapel (find) :   SO 060 624   LR 147   RA

Llandrindod Waterworks (find)

Construction work in 1911 was responsible for the discovery of two cinerary urns here, just behind the chapel. Although the site is across the river Ithon from Castell Collen fort, and a little downstream, it is alongside the presumed route of RRX 76. This, the highway east out from Castell Collen to Watling Street, is thought to have joined RR 621 just north of the practice camps, and to have crossed the Ithon as part of the road up from Brecon. If this was so, then the urns might well have come from a typical roadside cemetery.

One of the urns was represented only by some pale grey sherds, but the other was a splendid vessel. It can be seen in Llandrindod Wells Museum: a big, dark pot with high shoulders and inset handles. Inside it was human ash and bone, and on the polished upper part of the urn was written ATTILLI.

The original description (by M.E.Cunnington, in *Archaeologia Cambrensis*, 1911) says: "It might be read, therefore, as 'of Attillius', that is to say 'the ashes of Attillius'!" It is sobering to think of Attillius as a living man: one who died here, and whose buried remains were exposed as a curiosity. One of the changes that has overtaken

Alas, poor Attillius...

archaeology recently is in attitude to the ancient dead. When practicable, remains are now decently reburied; but it was not always so.

Llandrindod Fortlet : SO 055 601   LR 147   RA

What appears to be a fortlet, rather than a practice camp, is just perceptible as a dim rectangle in the first field on the north side of the lane which leaves the A 4483, crossing the railway at SO 056 600.

The Practice Camps and the road are just beyond the fortlet, along the same lane. This is private land with little parking space (dogs not allowed). The signposted field-track running south-west behind Castalia actually crosses the RR 621. The agger appears as a flat platform half-way across the second field, over which the wire fence passes. This is perhaps the most substantial, visible bit of accessible Roman road in the area, that has no subsequent track or path overlying it. It is really worth seeing.

Llandrindod Common

Practice Camps: SO 053 600 to 056 604   LR 147 RA

A terminological exactitude - the Imperial army really did practise making camps. The military reasons were good: the safety of a unit marching in hostile territory across the vast regions of diverse nations conquered and occupied by Rome was always at risk when the troop was resting. The army's ability to halt and create a precise, pre-designed defensive camp which needed no discussion, no planning and virtually no orders was as significant a weapon as any catapult or shield-formation. Consequently this vital skill was practised when the army was in barracks, and such camps are still to be found near most of the forts. It was as much a part of military training as cavalry exercise or target practice.

Tacitus has an awful anecdote about a new commander arriving with his unit in the middle of a Syrian winter. Authority, discipline, fortitude etc. being obviously at stake, the unfortunate legionaries were put to building practice camps. The sentries, says Tacitus calmly, froze to death, standing rigidly on guard, and the hands of men bringing in firewood snapped off their arms as they dropped their loads. The while the new commander skipped around in scanty garments in a frenzy of nervous energy.

It is unlikely that it was ever quite that bad on Llandrindod Common, but certainly things went to extremes here, for no less than eighteen camps have been recorded in a group. Ten of these are either now destroyed, or have only ever been seen from the air. The eight which have any presence on the ground are Scheduled Monuments under the protection of Cadw (the full list, with grid references, is available in the National Monuments Record).

Only one can really be seen easily without leaving the metalled track. In the field immediately west of Castalia, on the south side of the lane, the outline of the western half of Camp XII (OS and RCAHMW number; Cadw Camp E) is a well defined bank. The next camp south beyond it (XIII; F) is obscured by the rise of the slope, but almost opposite, on the north side of the track, faint heavings outline another camp (XI; D). The remaining sixteen lie to north and south...

West of the Practice Camps, the RR 621 runs under the modern town straight to the Ithon. Here it is thought to have been joined by RRX 76, to cross the river and ascend to Castell Collen fort.

Llandrindod Wells Museum : LR 147   RA

This is a friendly and helpful local museum in the centre of the town, which houses the Castell Collen finds. It is undergoing reorganisation, but anticipates presenting an even larger permanent exhibition of the Roman material by summer 1995, including the more massive stone inscriptions. As it is, all the most lively and attractive small finds are on display already, including a set of Castor-ware cups and a love-ring (see below, Castell Collen Fort). Refreshingly, the present exhibition concentrates on the material itself, rather than filling up the space with illustrations and texts at the expense of unique objects as has, regrettably, become the fashion.

A very interesting information sheet, written by the senior librarian, is available (free) from the town Library and from the Tourist Information Office next door to the museum (also very helpful to the Roman-tripper). This gives a detailed history of the excavations at the fort, with full references, and is well worth having when visiting Castell Collen.

Castell Collen Auxiliary Fort : SO 056 628   LR 147   RA

If ever a Roman fort had romance, this is it. Engrossed in huge trees, and laced by twisted roots, the massive rampart banks bleed out revetment stones, laid by men of the Second Legion Augustus, into the nettles and buttercups. Thistles and couch-grass, mosses and a twisted thorn gentle the strange, rhythmic wall-lines, once *Praetorium, Principia, Horreum*. The trees cast deceptive depths of shadow that obscure the full extent of the fort and isolate it from its dramatic position high up above the Ithon. The gateways are half-closed by heavy branches, and the ditches awash with fern and heady grass.

Although a Scheduled Monument with right of access, the fort is not signposted. To reach it, take the lane to Cwm Farm, running north from the A 4081, and follow it north and then east to Castell Collen house. There, go through the paddock to the left of the house; the fort is on the right, behind the garden.

Castell Collen has been admired for generations. On Thursday 25th August, 1910, eighty members of the Cambrian Society travelled in seven carriages and four motors to visit the remains. Seven months later the first excavation was opened. This first examination, in 1911-13, concentrated on the central, administrative block, and the second, in 1954-7, on the gateways and extra-mural baths.   The plan reproduced opposite was published in 1964, and shows both the structures discovered on the earlier occasion and the trenches opened in the fifties Unfortunately, of the later sessions only interim accounts were ever published, and no full archaeological report appeared. However detailed analyses of the finds have

61

CASTELL COLLEN, RADNORS.

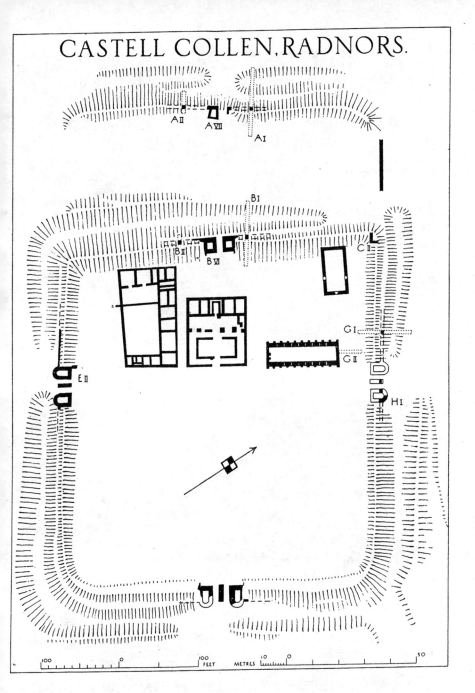

Reproduced by kind permission of Professor Leslie
Alcock and the editor of *Archaeologia Cambrensis*.

Castell Collen, east rampart.

Old Quarry, Beguildy, north Radnorshire.

been produced by the experts in each field concerned.

Castell Collen was originally a turf and timber work of considerable size, which was built during Frontinus' wars against the Celtic hillsmen. At this stage it was the size of all the remains visible today: that is, it extended out to the 'extra' bank which was, in fact, the original west rampart of the full-size fort. The first ditch was W-shaped (a particularly malicious design, intended to break the ankles and overbalance the desperate strugglers down there in the mud and blood). The west ditch seems to have been deliberately water-filled, but elsewhere stake-holes were found in the inner angle of the ditch-bottom. These were explained as a system of small sharp pegs designed to penetrate the soles of the barefoot Ordovices - a device known as *cheval-de-frise*, and also possibly used at Caerau (q.v.). Five feet back from the lip of this fearful ditch, the rampart faces were based on cobbles revetted with turf and topped by a timber palisade. A wooden watch-tower guarded each corner, and there was a timber-built entrance in the centre of each of the four ramparts. Outside the defences, the baths were built beyond the south-east corner. Their position can be located by standing on the corner of the fort diagonally opposite to, and furthest from, the modern house. In the field beyond there are two big shade-trees. The baths site is just this side, and to the right, of the left-hand tree, on the edge of the scheduled area. Under the baths, the fifties' excavation revealed an early occupation site which, it was suggested, might have been a labour-camp for the builders. Inside the fort, apart from the remains of wood among the packing stones in postholes found below the *Principia*, there is no record of the earliest administrative block. A handful of small Samian sherds from this period, and a very battered stud inlaid with silver, and possibly from a grandly studded belt, were found in the *Praetorium* site, from where several coins of the same, Vespasian, date were also recovered.

After this initial occupation Castell Collen seems to have been quite abandoned - perhaps because Agricola really had perpetrated the genocide Tacitus claimed for him. In the reign of Antoninus (AD 138-161) the legionaries came back to the deserted fort, and the reconstruction of Castell Collen in stone at the same date as that suggested for the refortification of Brecon Gaer poses the same question: were they extra quarters for troops brought down from the completed Wall, or for reinforcements needed to face rebellion from resurgent hillsmen?

There are three Building Stones from Castell Collen, but none of them is reliably dated. One, RIB 415 (now in Carmarthen County Museum, Abergwili), declares that the Century of Marcus (or Marcius) built forty-five feet. [Marcus is too common a name to make a neat connexion with the Marcus whose Century built at Tomen-y-Mur, a large and elaborate complex on the western coast-road in Caernarfonshire.] The second stone, RIB 416, is in a neighbouring church at Llanbadarn Fawr, RA (q.v.). Scarcely more helpful is a commemorative stone, RIB 414, of the type raised over a doorway. This has little left beyond two Ps. It has been suggested that these might stand for P(atri) P(atriae) ("father of his country"), indicating the presence of *LEG II AVG* in Trajan's time, when this formula was most often used; and that the *Principia*, from which it may have fallen, was rebuilt first.

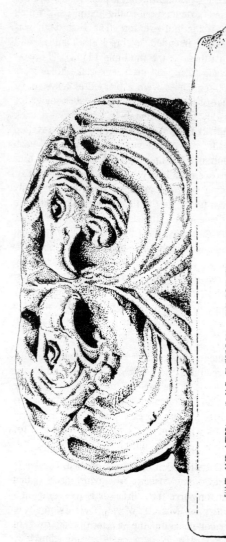

The second fort was a hugely impressive, full-blown edifice, with stone-work by *LEG II AVG*. The nasty ditch was deepened and widened, the ramparts were heightened and faced with dressed limestone, and the new double-arched gateways were the grandest yet built. The west gate at Brecon Gaer (also by the Second Legion) had already been designed with projecting gatehouses, but at Castell Collen three of the four gates were given massive, rounded defences: among the first in Britain to be raised in a style which endured for over a millennium as the ultimate in efficacy and magnificence. The Praetorian (east) Gate was probably embellished by the legion's Building Stone, inscribed with their titles and emblems, supported by eagle-eyed double griffins. The discovery of two ferocious spear-heads (one eight and a half inches long) and a peculiarly vicious-looking sling-bullet (one and a half inches long and weighing three and a half

Double griffins enhancing the side of the dedication stone. This carried an inscription to the detachment of the Second Legion which probably built the great gates.

ounces) shows that the scale of the rebuilding was not just ostentation.

Immediately inside the North Gate, and very vivid on the ground, are the remains of the granary (*horreum*). The outline of the actual building can be seen - not tidy and preserved, but overgrown and lined by clumps of juncus standing in the hollows of the old excavation trenches. A rounded heap of excavation soil now fills the central area, which once held the tonnage of grain. Ninety-three feet long, the granary stood lengthwise along the *Via Principalis*, and was an elaborate and ingenious structure. Inside, the granary floor was raised on a line of seventeen massive sleepers: part of the precautions taken against rats and mould. The walls were punctuated with ventilators, and around one were the marks of flames which had roared out of the interior in some appalling incident.

Granary wall as seen during excavation. Drawn from a photograph published in 1913.

At the other end of the administrative block, the *Praetorium* was a twenty-room affair equipped with a hypocaust and internal divisions of what seems to be plastered wattle-and-daub, the whole built around a large courtyard. Peculiarly, it is not quite aligned with the ramparts or the *Via Principalis*, which ran across the front of it from North to South Gates. There is evidence that some of the rooms at the back of the north range were re-shaped, but no clear description of alterations really emerges from the early accounts.

The seven dark 'Castor ware' cups (now in the museum) appear to have come from the range of five rooms across the back of the *Praetorium*. The lustrous, silky dark surface is a thin coating covering the pinkish body of the pottery, which was made in eastern England in the huge potteries of the Nene Valley (such ware is now usually known as Nene Valley ware). The gold point of a pin or writing stylus came from somewhere in the front, and a considerable amount of Samian ware from two small rooms in the same range. Perhaps it was through here that the handbell sounded its (reputedly unmusical) summons. The bronze chape (triangular end-piece) of a sword scabbard with fine open-work decoration, and a silver ring with *Amor Dulcis* ('sweet love') somewhat inelegantly inscribed on the outside both came from the house. A more aggressive vein is displayed by part of another splendid silver ring (something in the style of a knuckle-duster), of which only the projecting ornament remains. This (also in the museum) represents a pair of panthers - such as might be seen in the amphitheatre, and which were sacred to

Bacchus - on either side of an urn. A fine blue glass-paste gem engraved with a mounted god pursuing a snake-footed giant was lost from its setting somewhere around the house, and a lead phallus abandoned in the courtyard. All rather lively, and very Roman.

In the centre of the fort, at its very heart between the *Praetorium* and the granary, stood the *Principia*. This, as headquarters, shrine, martial court and assembly-halls all in one, was built on impressive, if standard lines. Two bronze brooches and a fine scabbard loop (nearly complete) in the shape of a swimming dolphin were found in its ruins, together with harness rings, nails, and the thin, patterned bronze hoop off the mouth of an expensive vessel. The shrine itself, which housed the eagles, the statues of god-emperors, sacred regalia and the unit's honours, faced out through a colonnaded hall, across the courtyard beyond, and straight down the ceremonial central street to the Praetorian Gate. A single, twisted thorn tree now stands on its threshold.

The extra-mural baths, beyond the south-east corner, were made remarkably grand by the presence of a large basilica-style exercise hall in front of the entrance. It is thought that this was lit by a multi-windowed clerestory, and had an overall roof carried on pillars which would have created an internal aisle-effect all round. The baths themselves consisted of a cold room with a cold plunge, a warm room with hypocaust below and an apsidal alcove to the south, a hot room where hot-water basins stood in an apse in the south wall, and finally a sweating room on the way out. At the end furthest from the exercise hall was the furnace room which heated the hypocaust underlying the whole suite of warm and hot rooms.

Like Brecon, the barracks at Castell Collen seem to have been made of wood throughout; and, also like Brecon, they appear to have been burned to the ground when the fort was side-lined. Indeed, the departing army may also have razed some of the walling themselves; the rest fell into grievous disrepair. When it was next needed, some time in the third century and after a second period of abandonment, the ditches had to be re-dug and the walls rebuilt. This time the army came back in greatly reduced strength. It was now that the *Retentura* was abandoned, and a new western rampart built directly behind the central block. The old bank was left standing as an outer bulwark, and in the new defences the single-lane gate, guarded by a wooden tower, was a beggarly thing compared with the hauteur of the older entrances.

It may have been in response to the same reduced circumstances that the great hall at the entrance to the baths was narrowed to almost half its previous width. The Praetorian and North gates were rebuilt, and this time the walls were re-faced with huge squared blocks and, in places, with stone-work in the well-known 'herring-bone' style. The great gate-houses were restored, and it is probable that it was now that the griffin-stone inscription, broken when it fell from its proud position, was re-used in the baths, to effect repairs to the floor there. Some of the finest Samian ware from Castell Collen is dated to this period, and a number of the more spectacular finds from the *Praetorium* and *Principia*. Coins give a date at which the fort was certainly in commission (193-217 overall).

Reorganisation of Britain's installations was undertaken by Constantius Chlorus, father of Constantine the Great, and an indefatigable road-repairer. The fort had once again been abandoned, and again the ditches had silted up and the stone-work sagged. But this time the repairs are far less sophisticated, and as much as is known seems to emphasise consolidation of a less spectacular, rougher station.

*

Route 8 : RR 623 - The Road from Llandovery (ALABUM) to Castell Collen

RR 623 is a major road running diagonally across Wales from MORIDUNUM (Carmarthen) in the south-west to BRAVONIUM (Leintwardine) on Watling Street. Both of these forts were strategically of the first importance, and both developed large associated civil settlements in their environs. The road comes into Breconshire at SN 850 420, half-way between Llandovery (ALABUM) and Beulah, which it links to Castell Collen in Radnorshire. The same road continues as RRX 76a to the modern border, just west of Leintwardine.

Abererbwll :   SN 849 415   LR 160   BR

This is probably a fortlet. The banks, enclosing half an acre, are quite visible on one side, but concealed by a plantation on the other. It was discovered by aerial photography, and has never been explored beneath the surface. It is on the east side of the forest track, not far from the picnic place. It is thought that it may be on some sort of link road to the north-west, which joined RR 623 from Llandovery to Castell Collen, but considerable efforts to locate this have so far failed.

It is always difficult, in the close hush of a coniferous forest, to imagine the fury and the noise which must have accompanied Roman battles. The British raised their adrenalin with the spine-chilling hollow lowing of the enormous battle-horns, the chiefs riding to the field in front of the fighting men, in fast-moving, iron-rimmed chariots, beating their spears against their shields. Opposite them, the Roman army marched, wheeled, advanced, manoeuvred, to the strident blasts of trumpets and a

---

cornet-like instrrument, on which riffs and winds blared their battle orders - all this apart from the natural noise of men and animals *in extremis*. Perhaps it is fitting that some of these places should be shrouded in silence now.

RRX 77 is another diagonal road linking Pen-y-Darren in the south (see RR 621) to Beulah, via Brecon Gaer. The suggested junction of RRX 77 with RR 623 is at SN 920 470, where RR 623 fords Afon Irfon at its confluence with Afon Dulas.

Nowhere along its route is it visible, nor is there any direct archaeological evidence for it. Adventurous Roman-trippers are advised to leave it alone - most of it is in the gun sights on Sennybridge Artillery range.

Llangammarch Wells (find) : SN 936 473   LR 147   BR

Two coins have been saved from a hoard buried in an urn which was found at the railway-station in 1872. Dating from the dark times of Victorinus, one of the 'Gallic' Emperors (269-71), the find is yet another case of a deposit account which misfortune prevented the owner from ever reclaiming.

The construction of railway networks at the end of the last century revealed a mass of archaeological sites all over Europe, and a great number of 'find spots' simply record such an episode. Today, it is the aim of archaeological trusts to investigate any chance finds or remains which building work, road-laying, ferreting or ploughing may turn up. This 'rescue archaeology' often turns into a race against the bulldozers.

A long stretch of road, from SN 920 470 to 923 506, has been proved to overlie the Roman road between the Irfon and the Cammarch. Its uncanny straightness and wide verges give it a weird authenticity. [See the photograph on page 41.]

Dol y Gaer (find) :   SN 92 48   LR 147   BR

About 1700 Edward Lhuyd noted "a curious Cornelian seal found near Dole Y Gare, late in ye possession of Mr. Steadman." Since the farm is on the side of the road, only a mile from a major fort, and since the Romans were extremely fond of carnelian intaglios, it seems fair to include this as a likely 'find' spot.

Route 8

Beulah Practice Camps

also known as

Llwyncadwgan Practice Camps : SN 9200 4995 LR 147 BR
SN 9209 5017

Both of these have been seen in aerial photographs, but there is no trace of them on the ground.

Beulah Marching Camp : SN 919 507 LR 147 BR

A vast temporary camp of over thirty-six acres lies in the rough pasture between the Roman/modern road and the A 483 to Llandovery. It is best seen by walking the six fields in which it appears. Parts of the west and much of the north side, including the in-turned clavicular entrance, appear as low banks. The nearest farm is Llwyngwilym, to the south-west of the camp. A fair sample of the indistinct nature of the remains can be gained by peering over the roadside hedge from the A 483 just outside Beulah, on the Llandovery side.

The Killing Fields of Caerau : SN 923 502 LR 147 BR

Caerau Fort, Beulah Fort (by Twdin Motte).

Just across the road from the marching camp, this sinister fort and its civilian *vicus* survive as gentle folds in the sheep fields around Caerau farm above the Cammarch river. Once again, the Normans found the locality of sufficient tactical significance to warrant a *motte*, and the availability of plentiful hard-core in the old defences may have led them to the site on the south-west rampart.

The farm and its vegetable garden are built inside the fort, beside the *motte*. The area

B	? Baths
F	Fort
K	Killing Field
M	Marching Camp
P	Practice Camps
V	*Vicus*
*	Best viewing places

covered by the fort and *vicus* lies between the road (ancient and modern), the river and the farm. Permission to visit the fields must be sought from the farm; but perhaps the best place to pick out the low ridges is from the Beulah-Garth road, A 483, between Black Bridge and Maesllech lane. From here there is a good view of the site of the fort and settlement. One dull evening, staring despondently at this blank hillside, I was about to label the site as 'invisible' when a sudden shaft of low evening sunlight slanted across the fields and, like something in a child's pop-up book, the whole plan of the fort appeared in 3-D. Such trickery of light and shade is well known to field wanderers, and never fails to chill the spine with awe.

Sherds of datable Samian ware and coarse pottery datable to c. AD 70-95, show that the earliest fort defences were constructed during the Conquest, probably for a unit of five hundred infantry or cavalry (*quingenaria peditata* or *quin. equitata*). The ramparts were made of clay, set on a clay or cobble footing and faced with turves. Outside these, double ditches surrounded the fort enclosure, and an outer ditch continued on, taking in the 'killing field'. It is the absence of a bank around this area that distinguishes it from sites like Castell Collen and Coelbren, where an 'annexe' was enclosed within a great rampart. This 'killing field' gives Caerau a sinister ambience - a visible relic of proud Ordovices enticed across the single ditch, becoming trapped between it and the implacable defences before them, and going down in organised butchery. Not that the concept would have been shocking to them - there are instances of a variety of 'killing field' around Celtic hill-forts; but there is something about the precise geometry of this brutal little rectangle that chills the blood.

In Trajan's time (98-117) a higher rampart and single ditch replaced the earlier works. A civil settlement developed outside the north-east wall, leaving a litter of pottery and building material under the sod. Test-pits dug in 1970 found four possible floor platforms, and one much larger floor, perhaps of a public market or hall; but nowhere is any of the *vicus* upstanding or even visible to the eye. However there is a noticeable 'ledge' on the north-east side, beyond the killing field. Bricks and tiles found here suggest that it may have been the fort's bath-house. It can (always) be clearly seen both from the main road and from the overgrown stile beside the south-west pier of Black Bridge. [The footpath indicated as crossing the field from here shows no sign of life.]

Caerau was abandoned (dismantled?) when the troops were moved north to the Wall by Hadrian or Antoninus Pius. The *vicus*, however, continued to flourish for much longer, which argues for considerable security for Romans and Romanised civilians in the area. Presumably the killing field had done its work.

The RR 623 passes to the west of the fort, at which point signs of building foundations (probably part of the vicus*) have been seen below the verges of the overlying modern road. Beyond the fort, the Roman road descends sharply to the*

Cammarch. Here the modern road swerves to meet the main road, but RR 623 continues under the swampy ground on the east side. Having forded the river it changes direction and drives north-west, straight up the hill. Its foundations (three feet of rammed stone on clay) and a Samian sherd have been discovered in the fields. Under some conditions it does show up on the hillside; and from the road above, at c.SN 930 513, it appears as a slight heaving in the line of the field-bank immediately south-west of the little by-road leading east out of Beulah village.

From here it heads across country to Glandulas, and has been proved by recent field investigations, aerial photographs, and sightings of the causeway at several points along this stretch.

The road is not visible at the Wye. On the breast of the hill due west of the crossing there is a farm called 'Sarn Helen'. Aerial photographs have picked up the road running straight across the high ground behind it, towards the river. It is quite a jolt to see that name hand-painted on a board on the windswept hillside. The farm across from it is called Pencaer Helen.

Penmincae Fortlet : SO 006 539   LR 147   RA

This was discovered in 1973 by aerial photography, and is really undetectable by the earth-bound from anywhere except the site itself. In severe conditions faint linear stains can just be perceived from the height of the hill on the right (south) bank of the river, looking from the road over Goytre wood (but when the trees are in full-leaf even this is no good). The fortlet is in the south-east half of the big field opposite the south-east end of the little mid-stream island - slightly higher than the surrounding ground. The banks, which are actually there, have to be seen from the river-side; permission must be sought at Penmincae farm. A gap indicates an entrance in the west side. Some sherds of Samian ware, glass, and pieces of an amphora have been found around the ramparts. A garrison here would hold the crossing and the section of the road between Caerau and Castell Collen.

The curving, sweeping banks of the river must have been a refreshing posting for men who spent so much of their time marching in straight lines to build straight roads and square camps, out of which they marched in a straight line.

The RR 623 continues NNW from Penmincae, where field-work has again indicated the route, to cross Gors y Llôn Nature Reserve. This is not open to the public; for special permission contact The Warden, Countryside Council for Wales, Penllyn, Cathedine, Bwlch (Tel. 0974 730751). The Roman road lies to the west of the modern footpath through the Reserve. From here on it has not actually been sighted; the route has been deduced. Bearing this in mind, it can (in theory) be picked up again as the farm lane leading from the north side of the bog to the A 470 at SO 018.562. Opposite the lane entrance, across the A road, the Roman road reappears in the paddock on the north side of the small-holding's yard.

It runs due north, parallel to the stream, on a perceptible terrace until it reaches the hedge. Here it turns north-west for Rheol. A footpath, which suggests that it might be possible to follow the road onwards, is indicated by a sign on the roadside, but comes to a sudden death on the other side of the hedge. Tantalisingly, its course is visibly appreciable from the surrounding road and lane banks, running diagonally through the fields until it emerges at the end of the lane at Rheol farm, beside the marked bridle-path. Here it continues amongst scrubby thorn bushes and alignments of hedge-banks (SO 026 568). The next fair view is the first stretch of the drive leading to Bryn. This leaves the by-road at SN 045 584, west of the railway, and the beginning of it is on RR 623 (the evocative gated lane at the end of this length is, alas, just west of the Roman line).

RR 623 joins RR 621 north from Aberyscir, somewhere near Lower Gaufron (SO 040 570).

A quite different route used to be suggested, taking the RR 623 out to the west from Beulah, through Newbridge and Llanyre, and running into Castell Collen from Cwm Farm, where the line was lost. Nearly all of this route travels along by-roads, and none of it has been archaeologically proven.

Route 9 : RRX 79 - The Road west from Castell Collen to the West Coast

The road north-west from Castell Collen is assumed to have run through the rolling agricultural hills between the fort and the Black Brook, where that stream joins the Dulas. There is no physical evidence anywhere for its route, but the presence of two military stations shows that there must have been a road somewhere. The A 44 joins the hypothetical Roman line just west of Nantmel, the modern road having run along the north bank of the Afon Dulas, whereas the Roman road took a route south of the river. RRX 79 is assumed to underlie the A 44 the rest of the way to Rhayader.

Llwyn Farm (find) : **SO 029 677   LR 147   RA**

Nantmel

A quernstone which may be either Roman or Iron Age was ploughed up in the late 1970s. The field where it was found is about a mile north of the presumed Roman road and the fortlet. The stone from Llwyn Farm is grooved with a series of lines designed to capture the grains and spill out the fine flour; this slim, elaborate form is most unlikely to have been in use in mid-Wales before the Conquest. Although it could itself be post-Roman, the stone may mark the introduction of Roman agricultural practice into an area where the Roman presence was strongly felt. At all events, it is just such a stone as would have been used where Roman techniques were adopted or enforced.

Dolau Fortlet : SO 0190 6654   LR 147 · RA

also known as **Nantmel Roman Fort**

Low banks running diagonally through the heavy pasture are all that can be seen of the ramparts and walls of Dolau. The fort lies under the corner field where the by-road to Nantymynach joins the A 44. There is plenty of easy parking on the wide verge of the main road, and a few yards along the side-road, a hop up on to the hedge-bank gives a good view of the shadowy remnant of the south-western defences. The field is on the curve of a slight hill, and the south-eastern bank is not really visible. The steep scarp which cuts off the north-east side - very noticeable from the main road - is recent, and nothing to do with the edge of the fortlet, which would have come out into the path of the A 44.

Dolau was a small station, the only 'fortlet' in the region, and it has been suggested that it was intended rather for a unit on exercises than as a permanent or belligerent post. A wide ditch, and a bank nearly three metres across, were discovered in a small, verifying excavation in the mid-sixties, however no datable evidence was found. 'Dressed stones' were said to have been turned up by the plough, but their relevance to any Roman remains has been discounted, since no sign of a stone-built, or indeed any internal structure was recovered.

Nantmel (find) : **SO 0082 6790   LR 147   RA**

Neuadd Llwyd/Noyadd

Another quernstone, this time the lower part, is recorded as having been found at the farm of Neuadd Lwyd on the hill above the Black Brook. It was seen there in 1911.

Rhayader (find) : **SN 976 681   LR 147   RA**

A complete quern, upper and nether stones, was found when drainage was being laid near the town, around 1880. This was a large piece, the upper stone forty-four and a half inches in circumference, with a handle-hole in the side. This stone, which appears in the indices as a possible Roman or Iron Age find, is recorded as lost.

The suggestion has been made that Rhayader itself may be the site of a fort. Its situation on the Roman road, and the slightly mis-aligned cross-roads in the heart of the town, have been taken as indications of a Roman ancestry. It was said that ramparts were found surrounding the town centre, but these have not been seen in any recent building or road works. A fort here would be very close to Dolau, if it was contemporary.

To the south of the town, Gwastedyn Hill rises abruptly over the Wye, which has here cut a steep, narrow valley. This dangerous route was avoided by the Roman road, which took the gentler and safer course around the northern flank of the hill, through Gaufron. The modern A 470, however, braves the cwm.

Cerreg Gwynion Hoard (find)   : **SN 9735 6573   LR 147   RA**

Above the lay-by on this sharp bend in the A 470, towering quarry-faces rise sheer above the Wye: indigo and silver in the rain, oyster grey and pearl-pale in sunlight. Black cracks and crevices trace the swooping bedding-planes in the slate; and one such, in May 1899, spilled out a hoard of Roman gold.

The story is a good one. James Marston had been up among the rocks looking for foxes (presumably they had been taking lambs in the valley below) when, turning for home, he shoved his crowbar against one last boulder, to loosen it. No fox's earth behind, but ancient gold jewellery, tumbling out on to the scree... Robbers, it was said, had divided the spoils of crime; one, who had hidden his share in the rocks, fell upon misadventure, and the glittering prize had lain in the dark heart of the slate ever since. A Coroner's court was convened that July, and the jewellery was declared Treasure Trove: "...which articles were of ancient time hidden as aforesaid, and the owners could not now be known."

The treasure was immediately sent up to the British Museum, and was "promptly appropriated by the Crown". This, said an indignant Rhayader doctor, "emphasised the desirability of having a National Museum for Wales". The National Museum of Wales was founded in 1907; the Rhayader gold is in the British Museum. The case epitomises the insoluble problem of national and regional museum collections, and of the expense (beyond the means of smaller organisation) incurred by the conservation and security of unique artifacts.

The hoard consisted of gold rings (one with an onyx intaglio engraved with an

Impression of the Cerreg Gwynion jewellery.

ant), a number of pieces of a gold necklace set with carnelians, two parts of an intricately worked bracelet, snake bracelets and 'Hercules Clubs'. These last are pendant-style hanging 'mascots', much favoured by the Romans. [There are bronze ones from the legionary fort at *ISCA* which may have hung from belts or scabbard harness.]

Experts in Roman jewellery have shown the combination of the style of the gold-working, the tooth-like settings and the use of enamels in a gold wire frame to be exceedingly rare: unique to Britain. This indicates that the workshop which produced them was probably in Britain, but with a Roman workforce. The artistic tradition to which the ornaments belong is Roman, and there is no hint of any local, Celtic influence in design or workmanship. The few other pieces identified as having been crafted in the same centre come from as far afield as Birdoswald on the Wall, a child's grave at Southfleet in Kent, and Ashstead, Surrey.

The Dolau command may have been a tough and austere posting (even, perhaps, some sort of horrible punishment), but the discovery of the hoard so close to the fort would indicate that men of considerable wealth were not spared its rigours (compounded, in this instance, by the unfortunate offender's having his family's status-symbols stolen in darkest Wyeside). Equally, it might just be that the jewellery workshop itself was in this area. The jewellery is on permanent display in the British Museum, but the Romano-British gallery will be closed for reorganisation at some point in the mid to late 1990s. The Museum advises long-distance visitors to check by telephone that the gallery is open.

Cerreg Gwynion crags form the corner of a little triangle of fertile farmland between Rhayader and the confluence of the Elan and the Wye. Set among the stark hills which rise in tiers of gnarled sessile oak to the open upland, it is a secluded, neat area, rippling with Wye waters and precisely hedged. From here another quernstone has been recovered.

Neuadd (find) : SN 958 668   LR 147   RA

Noyadd

Part of the upper stone of a quern was recorded at a farm early in this century. Quite possibly Roman, the quernstone draws attention to the river valley, sheltered and wonderfully beautiful among the bleak mountains. It is piquant that it was the Romans who brought the violet, which grows so richly here, into the valleys of the British countryside.

The suggested southern route of RRX 79b is the road at the top of Neuadd lane. Well to the north of RRX 79, a length of Roman road was visible in 1981, just south of St. Harmon, and heading due north into the mountains. Designated RRN 6, nothing more is known of it other than this brief stretch from SN 981 706 to SN 982 709. A long stretch is marked on the map, not all of which has been verified as Roman. It is, frankly, not very easy to see from the road, even in optimum conditions.

This 'floating road' would seem to head into a series of twisting river-cwms and narrow passes leading towards the Severn, west of Caersws (Montgomeryshire). The fort there stands at the hub of a northern system of roads which radiate out from a major military complex at the Severn-Cerist-Carno confluence. A more typically 'Roman' route has been made out as RRX 58, going north from Castell Collen through Abbey-cwmhir and the suggestively named Bwlch-y-Sarnau (Pass of the Roads), and on over a cairn-strewn upland ridgeway across Banc Du to the Caersws settlements. It must be said that there is no evidence for RRX 58, and that only a few yards of RRN 6 have been sighted: but those few yards do head straight past the north-west corner of the marching camp at St. Harmon.

St. Harmon Marching Camp : SN 986 716   LR 147   RA

The outline of a camp slanting across the lane at Cwm-ys-y-rhiw house was discovered by aerial photography, and is really visible only to the wingéd. Near the head of a wide, windswept valley, it overlooks an expanse of rough upland pasture, some better land down by the river, and the obvious route north from Rhayader as far as the mountain barrier. Up there the Ordovices ranged, refusing defeat. It is difficult not to see the unfortunate Romans, alone at the end of their lost road, nervously nibbling their surcingles and staring glumly over the ramparts into the Ordovician rain-storms.

The camp lies with its long axis north-west/south-east across the lane on the edge of a steep slope down to the north. There is a low, blunt line running aslant the large stretch of enclosed rough pasture just south of the junction of the lane with the road, and a hint of the return of the south-east corner up against the wire fence of the small paddock. Then there is a little hiccough in the slope of the lane, just where that line would cross under it. From the far side of the valley, at about SN 981 727, there is a southerly view over the hedge in which the suspicion of a contour can be seen at this distance, but it vanishes into the hillside on closer inspection.

This is a site for the dedicated and the airborne - which is a pity, as it appears so promising on the map, with the road just beside it.

RRN 6 is virtually imperceptible without plunging through the fields to the stream, where its recorded line stops a few paces upstream (in-stream). Permission to explore this should be sought from Glan yr Afon farm, further down the main lane. The 'path' marked on the Land Ranger map follows the hedges and crosses the line of the western defences just inside the second field; but like the 'path', any sign of the camp has entirely gone from here.

The proven part of the road is up on the hillside, precisely south of this point in the river, but is not generally accessible, lying beyond the buildings at the end of the grassy track which appears to lead straight towards it. The simplest place from which to try to locate it is from the opening of this lane, which is set back from the road, near the top of the hill. An old water-course and a grassed-out lane confuse the view from a distance.

Beyond the point where any postulated road leading towards St. Harmon would have branched off to the north, RRX 79 is presumed to have taken much the same route as the A 44 into Rhayader.

Rhayader Museum (East Street) : LR 147 RA

This is a small but developing local museum which is privately run and open only in the summer months. It has a collection of four splendid, well displayed and labelled quernstones, about which the curator is knowledgeable and enthusiastic. No description of the farming practices of the Roman period is meaningful without an image of querns, and this is a fine exhibition of the varieties and styles used in the area.

"What man is there of you, whom if his son ask bread, will he give him a stone?" (Matt. vii, 9). Yet to make bread he must first have the stone - a quernstone. Querns are the handmills which ground the cereal grains into flour. As the stones are large and often rather plain, they tend to lurk around on museum floors like deserted pedestals that some glamorous hero has vacated. In fact they are themselves the heroes, more significant than any individual Augustus: they ground the grain which made the flour which made the bread, Staff of Life.

A Clutch of Querns.

1. Rotary quern found during road-works undertaken in 1978, embedded in soil in South Street, Rhayader, at SN 972 678. This is not the 'lost' quern noted above.

2. Beehive quern found up beyond St. Harmon (also beyond RRN 6 - see p. 71) at Cnych Mawr Hill, SN 99 76.

3. The grooved stone from Llwyn Farm (see entry above).

4. Part of a rotary quern found in the bakery at Liverpool House, Rhayader. Its original provenance is unknown.

(All on display in Rhayader Museum. Drawing not to scale.)

The earliest querns were shaped like a saddle-seat, and the grains were ground by a separate rubbing-stone worked over them by someone kneeling or squatting. [The knack of making enough flour for even a small doughnut without incurring spinal injury is an acquired skill.] This type was used by the earliest farmer-bakers in the time of the first chambered tombs, right down through prehistory until an unidentified date which, in the remoter regions of Wales and Scotland, may have been as late as the Conquest. Other shapes came into Britain during the Iron Age, and were used by less isolated Celtic communities before the Conquest. These were rotary querns (flattish) and beehive querns (igloo-shaped). Both consisted of paired stones, of which the upper one was turned clockwise and anti-clockwise on top of the lower, crushing the grain between them. This was slightly less tedious and back-breaking than the push-and-drag action required by a saddle-quern. Incidentally, some of the gross wear found on the grinding teeth of ancient bread-eating populations has been attributed to minute grains of sand, quartz and so on, assimilated in the flour which came from the quernstones.

Although the Romans invented large mills using water and donkey-power, they brought nothing new with them in the hand-quern line. However they had made the basic designs lighter and more efficient, and the refined forms which they introduced were not supplanted for a millennium and a half. This means, of course, that a quern find is almost impossible to date closely if it has no other archaeological context.

Rhayader Museum has four splendid examples, all of which could be from Roman or Roman-British contexts, but none of which is directly datable. They are all isolated finds. The Museum has an excellent information sheet about querns, which describes in detail how they were used, with reference to the four on display.

RRX 79 is assumed to have divided, either at Rhayader or further to the north west, into RR 79b, heading for the fort at Trawscoed (Cardiganshire), and RR 79a, leading up to the station at Cae Gaer (Montgomeryshire).

Two ways have been suggested for RR 79b to cross the mountains towards the great western coast road (RR 69), which runs from Caernarfon (SEGONTIUM) in the north to Carmarthen (MORIDUNUM) in the south, like a westerly mirror-image of Watling Street, far off in the eastern Marches. The suggested southern line of RRX 79 runs down the Elan valley and out across the mountains along what is now a series of high mountain tracks passing through Cerrigwalau and the Claerwen Reservoir. From this drowned valley the route goes west across the mountains between Llyn y Gorlan and Nant Egnant. The northern option leaves Rhayader by the Mountain Road to the west of the town, and a car can be taken as far as the fork at Pont yr Elan. Here an old road, now a mountain path, tracks across the mountains to Afon Claerwen, where it would link with the path suggested for the southern route. It is marked, just uphill of the bridge, where a car can be left, by two pairs of whitened posts, and runs westwards across the flank of Esgair Rhiwlan, overflown by buzzards and stained by foxes.

Once again, there is no dating evidence for the origins of these very ancient mountain ways. These are tough walks, not surely Roman, and can be bitterly cold, with rapid, alarming weather changes - one thing to a disciplined, fully equipped cohort, but not for strolling along without company when the clouds come down... This is compass, maps, and serious boots country.

Esgairperfedd Marching Camp : SN 924 698   LR 147   RA

This is an enormous square of low rampart buried deep under the sedges and tussocks of storm-thrashed uplands. It covers fifteen and a half acres of coarse grass, juncus and reeds. In summer, when the vegetation is high, Esgairperfedd can be very elusive indeed, but under more spartan conditions it will reveal itself. Almost all of its bank can be followed, and the entrances seen quite clearly.

The following directions presume low vegetation (frost would be best, but makes the road tricky and the ears blue). The Mountain Road, signposted to Aberystwyth just south-west of Rhayader, climbs up out of the valley past a flight of waterfalls. [Vegetius, a Roman military writer, has a hearty remark about soldiers being best trained by "sweating and gasping". No doubt he would have approved of Esgairperfedd.] At SN 928 699 a wide, rutted track leads off the west side of the road, down to a ford across the river, and up to a complex of sheep-pens made of gates and corrugated iron. Multiple deeply scored paths and hollow-ways curve uphill south and then west from the pens, and vanish over the shoulder of the hill. This is marked on the map. From behind the pens another, unmarked, narrow footpath runs like a thin scar north west, almost parallel to the road and the stream. The north-east corner of the camp is twenty-five yards along here. The path continues north west in a straight line along the contour; the camp bank runs due west, aslant and up the hill. This is the north bank, and its in-turned clavicular entrance is ten yards further on. In the spare half of the year, this can all be seen from the roadside, a hundred yards or so beyond (north-west of) the beginning of the track, but in summer it vanishes into the natural waves of heavy growth.

Once found, the banks are not difficult to follow; it is finding the first corner that can be a problem when the grasses are high. The north bank ends in the first heavy clump of coarse sedge, where it makes a corner with the west bank. This appears as a bleached-out ridge, well below the small, bracken-covered scarp. The south-west corner vanishes into a swampy mire, but the south bank is apparent as another pale, thinly covered ridge, rising out of the bog and disappearing into the jumble of deep tracks and ruts coming up from the sheep pen. There is a clavicular entrance in all four sides, and all of them are detectable; those in the east and west banks are centrally placed, those along the north and south sides are much closer to the lower, eastern edges of the camp, approximately opposite each other.

It has been observed that although the marching camp appears to be in a hideously exposed area, its immediate siting is such that it gains maximum shelter from the prevailing winds. Typically, it lies on a small hillock between two streams.

Beyond Esgairperfedd, the Roman road made its way across the mountains by an unknown route to the fort at Cae Gaer, on the Rhayader-Aberystwyth road. The mountains in this area are rich in metal ores, including silver, although none of the mines has been irrefutably proved to have been worked in the Occupation.

✳

Route 10 : RRX 58 - The Missing Road North from Castell Collen to Caersws

Beyond the north gates of the fort, there is no trace of the road which surely must have existed to link Castell Collen to the significant valleys of the Severn and Carno. There, Caersws fort crouches in the heart of Wales and, like Brecon Gaer and Castell Collen, is another hub in another radial system of routes.

The little stretch of RRN 6 at St. Harmon (q.v.) could perhaps have struck across the hills eastwards to Bwlch y Sarnau (Pass of the Roads). Or it could have run west towards the fort at Cae Gaer, beyond Llangurig. Or it could have followed the approximate line of the modern B 4518, emerging on known Roman roads perhaps at Trefeglwys. Perhaps...

RRX 58 is a postulated route with west and east alternatives at beginning and end, using the flanks and shoulders of the mountains above the dangerous, twisting cwms which snake among them. No places, these, for a tired unit to be trapped in perpetual rain, between steep, boulder-strewn inclines and swampy, wood-tangled gorges. The suggested routes follow alternative lines: westerly, from Castell Collen more or less due north across country, along what are now traces of tracks, past the cairn and standing stone on Camlo Hill, to just north-west of Abbeycwmhir; and easterly, as far as Llanbadarn Fawr below Crossgates, as part of RRX 76, and diverging north to follow the Clywedog brook to Abbeycwmhir. Both hypothetical routes run along - and presumably above - the brook to Bwlch y Sarnau, and westerly to Brondre Fawr Hill. Here a western arm might take the old, very straight mountain path past the cairns and stone circle up at Fowler's Arm Chair, and thence over to Blue Lins Brook, from where another straight track runs right across a huge windfarm (starker and more geometric than anything the Romans ever thought up) and down to the upper Severn valley more or less at Caersws. An easterly option would carry on from Brondre Fawr past David's Well to Llaithddu, and thence due north to the Severn. This is less marked by the shades of old mountain trails, but also considerably less awful for most of the way.

The scatter of Roman sites and stray finds between this RRX 58 and RRX 76, to its south-east, lie quite far east of these mountain routes. So far no information has been published about anything which can be said to lie on, or near, either of the postulated RRsX 58.

Bryn Hir (find) : SN 98 78   LR 136/147   RA

"...this most peculiar bronze article..", as it was originally described in 1895, was thought to be "a brooch or fastening for a mantle". Now seen as the twisted remains of a buckle, it is likely to be Roman rather than Bronze Age, as was first suggested. It was ploughed up in 1877 in a field, the exact site of which is not now known. This is perhaps unfortunate, as the grid square SN 98 78 lies five miles due north of the stretch of road known as RRN 6 (see p. 77).

It is maybe just as well that the inn which used to stand just beside RRN 6 is no more. It was called 'Labour in Vain'...

Maylord Farm (find) : SO 1800 7150   LR 148/136   RA

The upper stone of a rotary quern came from somewhere on this farm by the headwaters of a tributary of the Lugg. This type of quern was introduced to the Celtic population by the Romans, but was thereafter made and used for a great length of time. The Maylord quernstone need not be Roman, although it is worth remembering that there was considerable Roman strength in the lower Lugg valley (RRX 76).

Fron Meadow (find) : **SO 195 765   LR 148/136   RA**

Another upper stone (domed) from a rotary quern came from the steep slopes of the
south side of Beacon Hill, above a narrow side-valley of the Teme. This one has a
slot to hold a (lost) handle.

WANTED: one wall painting from one Roman dwelling. What it would be to have a
record of the Roman perception of the British countryside, such as those of the
Italian landscapes preserved at Herculaneum and Pompeii. [The great eruption that
buried these priceless works happened in AD 79, the year after Frontinus left
Britain.]

Beguildy (finds) : **SO 1860 7982   LR 148/136   RA**

('Church House Finds' - after donor, not site)

A few very interesting pottery sherds were found by the road which leads out of
Beguildy village towards the site of the ancient lead mines below Cefn Pawl. Dated
to the first to second centuries, one of the pieces is highly polished ('burnished').
This is a piece of imitation Samian ware, a pottery style developed in the big kilns in
the east of England, and not likely to be the (legal) possession of a vanquished
goatherd.

Rhoshay (find) : **SO 181 787   LR 148   RA**

and **Beguildy ?Settlement** : **SO 1809 7874   LR 148/136**

Old Quarry

If ever there was a place given over to the meeting of Naiads and Dryads with the
spirits of springs and sweet waters, this is it; and it is idyllic. It can be approached
(on foot) by the lane passing the yard of Careg-y-Fran. [It would be helpful to the
occupier to know that there are visitors in the lanes.] On the floor of the valley the
trees close over a shallow, shadowy ford and footbridge, where the water is clear
and very musical. Beyond, the lane divides, the right-hand fork continuing upstream.
The site is at the end of the other track, which goes almost directly south across the
river, uphill beside thin-limbed trees. Across the field, on either side of a little
stream, are the lumps and bumps of the activity that gives the site the name 'Old
Quarry'. [See the photograph on page 63.]

From here the first to second century 'Rhoshay' sherds were collected by the
owners of Rhoshay farm, along the hillside; it is taken that they indicate the site of a
Romano-British settlement. If the occupants were using the imitation Samian ware,
this would indicate that the 'settlement' was of considerable significance.

The Romans were great hunters - even the overwhelmingly literate Pliny went
boar-hunting on his estates. One of the named resources of Britain was

hunting-dogs, and it was the Romans who introduced the fallow-deer to this country, perhaps for sport in just such a landscape as Beguildy, beyond the militarised areas. In fact, although this is a very 'herdable' species, and probably kept in semi-harboured circumstances, its predations on the shrub layer must have been a factor in the clearance of low or secondary woodland. There is a delightful painting of a doe from Pompeii, but she has been appropriated by a goddess and is out of her natural habitat. The Romans also kept a huge number of goats - small, amber-eyed beasts shaped like a hirsute shoebox with lethal horns. Similar goats can still be seen, feral, on some Irish islands, where they have totally stripped anything even remotely woody. It is goats like these that give Pan his sinister look.

Beguildy Lead Mines : SO 1710 7983   LR 136/148   RA

The blocked adits, spoil heaps and rock debris of old mines clutter the floor of Stonehouse Dingle. This deep cleft is cut by a rapid little river, draining the south face of the hills above Beguildy. The gated track which runs southward from the crown of the hill is marked Private, but the site can be found by striking out among the sheep and horses, over the brow of the hill, and behind the enclosed fields. Sheep and rabbit tracks transect the waist-high bracken in summer (in winter it is likely to be a snow-field, and a bit uncomfortable), but there is no anthropophilic path.

Much has been made of the mineral wealth of the Welsh mountains, and the Romans' exploitation of it. The furnaces, bloomeries and slag of iron-workings have been found, but of the mines themselves there is little secure proof. Lead was another vitally important commodity to the Romans. The gigantic sections of lead water-pipes on display at Caerleon and in the National Museum, the lead coffins and bone-tanks to be seen there, the lead linings to the baths, and even the identity disks and seals used by the army and administration: all these give some illustration of its value. But the date of the mine is hard to prove. In a sense this is inevitable, as much of the ore must have come from surface workings, and even where adits were dug, most known mines were worked again in later centuries, thus removing and destroying all evidence of Roman activity. A further, and more unusual problem lies in the fact that prehistoric mining techniques tend to leave remains not easily distinguished from Roman working. The subject is fraught with difficulty, opinions are divided, and the journals full of conflicting arguments and hypotheses.

It is said of Beguildy lead mines that "the older portion is Roman"; and indeed, so it may be. Lead was being extracted from sites in Clwyd in Nero's reign, and the lower reaches of the Teme and Lugg valleys do contain some of the earliest military stations in Wales. This, and the number of Roman finds in the immediate locality would make the suggestion seem credible. However a major check to this excess of faith is the lack of any road known anywhere near the mine, and, significantly, of any garrison post to guard it and the convicts who would have worked it.

The mines were in use until the end of the last century. After they had been closed down, one of the redundant workers dreamed that there was gold deep in the blocked shafts. He spent the rest of his life looking for it. By day he panned for it in the rivers among the flowered-over spoil-heaps; by night he circled the district, taking the bars from his neighbours' gates to bind together into ladders, and exploding wicked cordite mixtures to shatter the secretive rocks. Alas, any clues to Roman activity which might have remained into the nineteenth century are unlikely to have survived such zeal.

Turgy (find) : SO 1623 8395   LR 136   RA

More Roman ware came from the steep slope above Nant Rhuddwr, now in the vicinity of a forestry track through Cefn Vron Plantation. This is yet another of the little valleys opening into the young Teme. In 1907 an urn was found, in 1927 an *olla* (a sort of jar), and twelve sherds were dug out of a deep badger's earth in the summer of 1929. The sherds were given to Shrewsbury Museum. Here again, these are real Roman objects: if not owned by Romans, then acquired directly from a Roman source, and evidence for more than the 'influence' of Occupation.

Trefoel Hill (find) : SO 1302 8000   LR 136   RA

An old rabbit warren was the find spot of some fragments of coarse grey cooking ware and sherds from at least four different vessels of red 'legionary' ware in the early fifties. In view of the affair of the Missing Road, this is an interesting position, high on the watershed between the Ithon and the Teme. A small excavation was mounted to investigate, but without result, since any helpful layers which might have been laid down in the soil had already been done over by bunnies.

Route 11 : RRX 76 - The Road East from Castell Collen to Watling Street at Leintwardine

The road out of the east gate of Castell Collen must have passed through the vicus *and down to ford the Ithon. From there it would join RRX 76 east to Watling Street. The Roman route is assumed to have followed that taken by the modern A 483, north to the church at Llanbadarn Fawr, just south of Crossgates.*

Crossgates Inscription : SO 088 644   LR 147 RA

Llanbadarn Fawr

RIB 416

This vivid inscribed Building-Stone came from the earlier structure of St. Padarn's Church. At the end of the last century, when the church was restored, the stone was built into the west wall of the porch. It is at eye-level, and quite clear, but the door opens across it so it is not immediately obvious. It reads: **c Val.Flavini** ("The Century of Valerius Flavius [built this]").

Just as the Building Stones at Tretower (q.v.) were ascribed to the fort at Pen-y-gaer, so this is taken to have come from the ramparts of Castell Collen. Ironically, this monument of the Conquest is gazed upon from the opposite wall by a carved *sheila-na-gig*, relict survivor of the Celtic civilisation Valerius Flavius fought to extinguish. Face to face, they co-exist in the queer light of twentieth century curiosity.

From here the line of the Roman road continues as far as Penybont, where it diverges south of the modern road and Llanfihangel Rhydithon, along a series of tracks and paths.

Dolau (find) : SO 14 67   LR 148   RA

In 1950 a Roman bead of a common type known as 'melon' was found just north of this stretch of the road, up on the hill behind the Manse. Our forbears seem to have made some arcane connection between the empire and the melon: they applied the term to a Roman hair-style as well. The bead was given to Llandrindod Wells Museum.

The road is thought to have forked at Bleddfa, the northern line (RRX 76a) going up through Knighton and on to the (now) English military sites at Buckton and Leintwardine, and the southern arm (RRX 76b) down the Lugg valley past Discoed, and on to Shobden in Herefordshire. Here it would be joined by RR 75 from Mortimer's Cross to Clyro (q.v.). [Bleddfa is another of the points where Scholarly Proddings have failed to strike an anticipated fort.]

RRX 76b to Mortimer's Cross

[Discoed : SO 2686 6528   LR 148   RA

Records and maps published in the 1970s may show a Roman fort here, however investigation of the site, revealed by aerial photography, showed that it belonged to a much later age and had no Roman connection whatever.

A great number of sites of all ages have been discovered through the application of techniques developed during the second world war. Several archaeologists of that generation, having worked in aerial photography during the hostilities, subsequently turned their skills to this most effective method of field search. Inevitably the occasional stain shows up which seems ancient but turns out to have been an outsize manure-stack or the relic of a W.I. marquee.]

Presteigne (find) : SO 31 64   LR 146   RA

A back garden in the High Street sprouted a coin of Maximian in the 1950s. Maximian, father of the Maxentius defeated by Constantine I (the Great), had a curious career. He had been Emperor of the western half of the Empire, and had retired as an elderly man; however in 306, when Constantine was declared Emperor in far-off York, Maximian was reinstated in Rome - one of several politically unsettling events with which Constantine's reign began. It is odd to think of Romans by the Lugg reflecting on these imperial upheavals by the Tiber.

Corton House (find) : SO 319 632   LR 148   RA/Herefordshire

Altogether, over sixty coins have been found in this garden, one end of which is in each county. Twenty-four coins were discovered in 1941 (perhaps as a result of turning the pansy beds over to parsnips during the wartime shortages). Another coin, dated to AD 97, was found in June 1951, and a further seven (AD 97-169) that July. The coins were presented to Llandrindod Wells Museum. The wide date-bracket suggests a collector rather than a hoarder - collectors come in all epochs.

Broad Heath (find) : SO 338 635 LR 148 RA

Llanlago

Further along the line of the supposed route of RRX 76b, a rim-sherd from a flanged bowl datable to the second century came up in a flat field downhill from a system of strip-lynchets (usually formed by prehistoric arable techniques). The field has been under potatoes since the find, and therefore thoroughly turned over, but there seem to be no signs that this is anything but a stray discovery. Maybe a clumsy movement by a large hound or careless orderly resulted in smashed crockery during a travelling legate's picnic eighteen centuries ago?

From here the Roman road crossed the Hindwell Brook and led into what is now England. It is thought to have joined RRX 75 (see Route 1) near Shobden, to run into Mortimer's Cross.

RRX 76a from Bleddfa to Leintwardine

Cribyn Llwyd (find) : SO 2340 7030   LR 148   RA

Parts of two elegant vessels of late first century pottery were found on the side of Gors Cribyn-Llwyd hill in the mid-fifties. The area is now a plantation. Forestry tracks circle the steep hillside, overlooking the dingle, but none of them goes close to the find spot. One jar is represented by its rim and neck, the other (a flanged bowl) by its diagnostic rim.

Gwernaffel (find) : SO 264 704   LR 148   RA

A complete 'urn', dated to the first century, was recovered from a bank at the head of the little cwm behind and south of Gwernaffel Farm. RRX 76a is taken to have passed just to the north-west of the farm, crossing the modern by-road at the junction, and striking north-east towards Knighton along the beginning of the track opposite. Nothing suggesting anything more than a coincidental relationship between the two finds from Gwernaffel is known, but their proximity does contribute to an impression of early and thorough settlement of the district.

Knighton (find) : SO 2865 7233   LR 148   RA

The handle of a Roman 'jug' was found just to the north west of the Teme bridge in the late 1920s. It remained in private possession, and nothing is known about it except that it was five feet below the ground. Natural change, floodings and human interference with the river bank over the centuries make this quite credible. The possibility of a 'lost' fort under the town has been put forward on other grounds.

From Knighton RR 76a heads due east along the Teme across the modern border with England, past the Roman sites at Buckton, and into the great fort at Leintwardine.

It is a strange experience to come out of the western mountains, with their grim forts and punitive mines, on to the most famous of Roman highways. It is strange to walk among the mellow brick Lanes of Leintwardine, where the legions marched; to wander among houses called 'Roman Lea' and 'Bravonium'; to be told: "The Principia? *Oh, yes - just down there, under the butcher's shop..." Strangest of all, to round a corner and come face to face with the Street's name on a roadside wall:*

```
o   WATLING STREET   o
```

GLOSSARY (+ abbreviations used in the text)

agger : The solid body of a road. Usually made of several layers of graded hard-core, and bounded by a drain/ditch on either side.

amphora : Immensely tall, handled jar with rounded or pointed base. Mostly used for transporting and storing liquid commodities: oil, wine etc.

ansate : Lit.: handles. A mildly decorative element added to the sides of otherwise plain, rectangular borders - in effect like the two laterals of a Maltese Cross.

auxiliary troops : Troops raised from the native population of a conquered nation. Considered inferior to the 'legionary', who was a Roman citizen and voluntary career soldier, auxiliaries frequently fought in their own style, with their own traditional weapons. Should he survive a full term of service, an auxiliary automatically gained Roman citizenship.

berm : The flat strip of ground between the descending face of a ditch and the upright face of a wall.

Building Stone : Record stone inscribed with identity of builders, and set in walls, structures etc.

centurion : NCO in command of a 'century' - a unit of ten groups of eight men.

clavicula : A curved defence work, where the rampart on one side of a military gateway overlaps that on the other side, thus causing those entering to pass, contained and vulnerable, between two ramparts before gaining access.

'Conquest' : Here applying only to the Roman conquest.

dolphin brooch : A common Roman ornament shaped like a T, with the stem curved out in a bow, away from the garment - supposedly like the back of a leaping dolphin.

ECM + number : Reference to entry in *Early Christian Monuments of Wales*, by V. Nash-Williams.

horreum : A granary.

hypocaust : System of blocks dividing an under-floor area into channels along which hot air flowed from a furnace. Effectively, under-floor central heating.

mansio : Official Rest House/Guest House for the Imperial post and official ranking travellers.

mortarium (pl. mortaria) : Large grinding or mixing bowl, usually with lips for pouring liquids. Essential culinary equipment.

motte : Norman onwards. An artificial mound upon which the keep of a castle was raised.

NMR : National Monuments Record of Wales. Archive and library situated in RCAHMW (q.v.).

Praetorium : Official in-barracks residence, and sometimes offices, of the commanding officer. Often translated as 'Commandant's House'.

prata : Lit.: pastures. Here, official grazing-lands for horses and cattle belonging to the military.

Principia : Headquarters, comparable to a modern regimental HQ. Contained sacred and secular treasure, eagles (banners), shrines, martial court etc.

retentura : Half of a fort, situated behind the principal buildings. Less prestigious than the **praetentura**, which faced towards the *Principia, Praetorium* etc.

RIB + number : Reference to entry in *The Roman Inscriptions of Britain*, vol. I, by R.G. Collingwood and R.P. Wright.

RCAHMW : Royal Commission on the Ancient and Historical Monuments of Wales (Plas Crug, Aberystwyth, Dyfed).

Samian ware : Fine, silky, red table-ware, frequently with abundant stamped decorations. Mass-produced in east and central Gaul at a number of known potteries and workshops, and exported all over the Empire. Makers' names are often stamped on the pots. Designs include geometric/architectural elements, and both realistic and mythical beasts and animals, often in semi-narrative contexts.

vicus (pl. vici) : Native civilian village-type ward, organised on Roman lines by native administrators.

INDEX

FURTHER READING

Original Accounts of the Conquest

Tacitus: *On Britain and Germany*, trans. H. Mattingly (Penguin Classics, 1948. Written c. AD 98).

    The Annals of Imperial Rome, trans. Michael Grant (revised edition, Penguin Books, 1989. Written by c. AD 120).

The Letters of the Younger Pliny (trans. Betty Radice, Penguin Classics, 1963; written c. AD 102-110) provide some very revealing glimpses of what it meant to a Roman to be a Roman.

General

R.G. Collingwood & Ian Richmond: *The Archaeology of Roman Britain* (Methuen, 2nd edition, 1969).

R.G. Collingwood & R.P. Wright: *The Roman Inscriptions of Britain, vol. I* (Oxford, 1965).

Johnson, Anne: *Roman Forts* (Adam and Charles Black, London, 1983).

Margary, Ivan D.: *Roman Roads in Britain* (revised edition, John Baker, London, 1967).

Nash-Williams, V.E.: *The Roman Frontier in Wales* (revised edition, Michael Jarrett, University of Wales Press, Cardiff, 1969).

    Early Christian Monuments of Wales (University of Wales Press, Cardiff, 1950).

Salway, Peter: *Roman Britain* (Oxford History of England, I A; Oxford University Press, 1981).

Webster, Graham: *The Roman Imperial Army* (Adam and Charles Black, London, 1969).

Further Reading

Local

Royal Commission on Ancient and Historical Monuments in Wales: *An Inventory of the Ancient Monuments in Brecknock (Brycheiniog); The Prehistoric and Roman Monuments, Part ii* (HMSO, 1986).

Royal Commission on the Ancient and Historical Monuments of Wales and Monmouthshire: *Inventory of the Ancient Monuments in Wales and Monmouthshire, III: County of Radnor* (HMSO, 1913).

Boon, George: *The Legionary Fortress of Caerleon - Isca* (National Museum of Wales, Cardiff, 1987).

James, Heather: *Roman West Wales* (Rampart Press, Carmarthen, 1982).

All the above have full bibliographies and references to the sites and finds described in this book.

The journal *Brycheiniog* and the *Radnorshire Society Transactions* publish articles of archaeological and historical interest, and accounts of excavations carried out in the two counties. *Archaeology in Wales*, published annually by the Council for British Archaeology, has excellent short articles and notices of excavations, field and laboratory work. Major articles concerning Welsh sites appear regularly in *Archaeologia Cambrensis* and the *Bulletin of the Board of Celtic Studies* (BBCS); *Britannia* is the official organ for Roman Britain (and Kindred Studies), while the *Journal of Roman Studies* has international application.

The **National Monuments Record, RCAHMW** (Aberystwyth), has a manual index and site records, and full linear maps of the Roman roads in the area. These are open to the public for consultation. The **Clwyd-Powys Archaeological Trust** (7A, Church Street, Welshpool, Powys SY21 7DL) holds the county Sites and Monuments Record, and may be consulted by post, or personally by appointment.

Acknowledgements

The authors are wholly indebted to the
books cited above, and to the innumerable
works listed in their bibliographies, but are
solely responsible for the opinions expressed
in the present volume.

We are most grateful for the continuous help
and courtesy shown by the National
Monuments Record, and the Clwyd-Powys
Archaeological Trust; to the curators at
Abergavenny, Brecon, Llandrindod Wells
and Rhayader for opportunities to lurk and
work in their museums; and to the staff of
the British Museum and the National
Museum of Wales for additional
information. We are very grateful to
Professor Leslie Alcock and *Archaeologia
Cambrensis* for permission to reproduce the
plan on page 62, and to the many land-
holders who gave us tea, encouragement,
and permission to walk their land.